the way t

PERFOR

the way to... PERFORM
WWW.MODEFOR.CO.UK

By Tabby Kerwin

The way to... PERFORM

First published by Mode for... Publishing in 2023

Copyright © 2023 Tabby Kerwin & Mode for...

The Way to... PERFORM is part of

The PERFORM Experience ®

www.modefor.co.uk

Other books from Mode for...Publishing

The Three Ps: Possibility, Productivity & Performance

The Three Taboos: Cancer, Grief and Mental Health

The PERFORM Journal

Weddings on the Mind: Putting Wellbeing into Weddings

This book is a collection of seven sections (available as individual short books on Kindle or in eBook and PDF format) based on PERFORM; the positive psychology framework at the center of The PERFORM Experience ®, developed by Tabby Kerwin through extensive experience and research.

INDEX

About the Author

Tabby Kerwin is an award-winning mindset coach, best-selling author, speaker, facilitator, musician and mental health advocate and trainer.

Based on her knowledge as a trained performer and her own lived experience of depression, anxiety and grief following the death of her husband in 2018, brother in 2014 and father when she was 16-years-old, Tabby hosts open and honest conversations and coaching using her own philosophy of *The Three Ps: Possibility, Productivity and Performance.*

Grounded in positive psychology, as a facilitator and mindset coach Tabby walks through life with those who feel stressed, overwhelmed and anxious to help them PERFORM and move forwards with resilience, hope and happiness to feel calm, in control and emotionally fitter.

Tabby is the successful creator and director of her portfolio business Mode for... where experience, performance and wellness meet through creativity and learning. She is the creator of The PERFORM Experience ®.

www.modefor.co.uk

INTRODUCTION

Based on her philosophy of *The Three Ps: Possibility, Productivity and Performance,* PERFORM is the strategy on which to bring the philosophy to life and live a resilient, happy and emotionally fitter life and perform at your best.

PERFORM incorporates seven elements:

Possibility

Enjoyment

Resilience

Focus

Optimism

Relationships

Mindset

By implementing Tabby's ideas and utilizing the short exercises contained in this book, PERFORM helps you become emotionally fitter, feel happier and more confident, perform at your best and protect your mental health.

We need to shift the narrative around mental health to a protective one and PERFORM supports this concept by giving you inspiration and help to develop your toolkit of simple wellness tools that you can incorporate into your day to help you perform at your best in every area of personal and professional life.

Find it hard to make time to do things to improve and sustain your emotional fitness and get mind fit? By building your toolkit with a variety of tools and spending just 7 minutes at a time implementing them regularly, you will start to feel emotionally fitter and mentally healthier.

Let's PERFORM

Throughout this book you will find a collection of exercises or 'tools' which you can try and add into your wellness toolkit.

It's really important that we have a variety of tools at our disposal in order to build our emotional fitness and that we don't just become dependent on one thing.

Why? Because if we only rely on one tool, it can become a crutch and for some, even an obsession or in the worst case, an addiction.

Furthermore having a variety of tools increases our Dopamine levels. Dopamine is known as the *'happy hormone'* and can naturally improve our mood and motivation, with a higher level bringing more feelings of wellness - therefore making us trust all the more in the concept of becoming emotionally fitter and consequently, we take action.

POSSIBILITY

the way to... Create Possibility

"There is always light, if only we're brave enough to see it. If only we're brave enough to be it."
Amanda Gorman, the youngest inaugural poet in US history

We are storytellers and creators by nature. It's inbuilt into us since the earliest days of human life. So imagine being able to create your own world of happiness, satisfaction, success and abundance.

Abundance is a feeling of fullness and the notion of having more than enough. It is not greed, but a sense of appreciation of life in its fulness, of spirit, soul, wealth, joy, mind and body. We're not just talking about money and luxuries, but the idea of creating a world of possibility.

Sound possible? Or in your mind is wealth, money, health, happiness, success and love just for other people? It doesn't happen to you; you just feel unlucky, undeserving or unworthy?

Let me tell you that you are absolutely worthy of everything you want. You are absolutely deserving and it has nothing to do with luck. You hold all the cards; you have all the power.

... and it all starts with your mindset.

Mindset

What does that mean I hear you ask? You've possibly heard of *'having the right mindset'* or maybe even the terms *fixed* or *growth* mindset. A fixed mindset could be described as being set in your ways with no intention of changing whilst a growth mindset could imply you are open to change, learning and indeed, possibility.

In short, a mindset is a set of beliefs that helps us develop the map that leads us to our goals.

"A belief is a feeling of certainty about what something means." Tony Robbins, author and speaker.

Your mindset is a choice. It's not something you're born with and can't change, you absolutely have the control to adapt and address – to change your beliefs – and it's certainly your choice to approach everything with a good attitude if you want to be satisfied and experience abundance and success.

Hard things face us all in life; stress, grief, worries and more and often we can't control the situations we are faced with, but we absolutely can choose our mindset to deal with them; and that's your personal responsibility. We have the possibility to grow from every difficult situation.

It's not for someone else to do the work for you and make life easy. It's up to you to do the work and take the consistent action and when you align the possibilities, your energy and the action... Wow! That's when things begin to change!

The only thing standing between you and what you want is you... or more specifically your mindset! Simple... though simple doesn't always mean easy.

I know it isn't always easy to adopt a mindset that makes you certain things are possible. Let's get real, it can be tough and often we are battling those internal voices and our inner *chimp*! Check out *The Chimp Paradox* by Professor Steve Peters who helps you get your inner *chimp* under control!

Maybe start by giving it an identity so you can differentiate between your mindset and that of your *chimp!* I shall call mine Buster! Buster can be an utter [......] (complete with appropriate expletive!) and if I let him, he will sabotage my thoughts and mindset and make me believe I am not worthy and things are pointless and hopeless. Buster is a liar. He thinks he's protecting me because in his mind, difficult situations equals danger, but I know that's not true. Difficult actually equals possibility... lots of it... so Buster is often told to stand down and get back in his box, where, in the main he lives very happily!

Sometimes we are battling demons such as imposter syndrome or the fear of being judged or we're basing our future on what's gone in the past. It's often said those that experience depression are anchored in the past whilst those experiencing anxiety are focused solely on the future.

Learn from past experiences, have an eye on what's possible in the future, then root yourself in the present to do the work to bring those possibilities to life.

... and the opinions of others that may be a trigger for you? Well, in the wise game-changing words of my friend *"the opinions of others are not your concern."*

Your life is safe for you to live, share and enjoy in the exact way you want to, so make it full of possibilities and do the work to bring them to life, and when things get hard, take that moment to stop, reflect, rest and give yourself space to go again. It's not your job to live the life other people expect you to in a way that makes them feel comfortable. It's not your job to constantly please other people. It's not your job to make yourself and your life small because other people don't hold a big vision for themselves.

However, it is your job to create your possibilities by holding the vision of what you really want so strong that you can see, hear, feel, taste and smell it and then plan the action you will take to realize those huge visions. Give yourself permission to do this for YOU. Choose your mindset and have fun with it.

Let's PERFORM

Exercise #1

Hope Map

Spend the next seven minutes (or longer if you have time) considering the following exercise.

Think of three goals that you want to achieve in your life for YOU in the next 12 months.

1.

2.

3.

Next, think of three ways you can achieve those goals. What actions could you take?

1.

2.

3.

Now, for each goal identify three things that could get in the way of you making those possibilities a reality and meeting those goals and how will you navigate those potential hurdles?

1.

2.

3.

You've just created yourself a little hope map, based on your beliefs of what is possible for you and by considering what could get in the way and identifying a plan 'B' to navigate around those potential hurdles. Now it's time to follow that map.

What will be your first step?

Your Goals

There's no limit to the size of goal you set yourself. Why not try the above exercise for different time frames, such as six months, one year, three or five years and perhaps even think of some huge life changing goals or HUGGs as authors Andy Cope and Andy Whittaker refer to them in their book *The Art of Being Brilliant.*

A HUGG is a huge unbelievable great goal! HUGGs (and hugs) are good! Both versions bring possibility, hope and connection and I'm an advocate for them both!

The most important part of the exercise is not just to write down your goals and to plan the action you are going to take to reach them, but to make a note of the things that could get in the way and potentially try to derail your plans. When we know what the potential pitfalls could be, we can make a contingency plan; a plan 'B' or 'C' if you like!

Let's PERFORM
Exercise #2
Miracle Question

Think about this question for the next seven minutes and journal some ideas.

Q: If there was nothing standing in my way, what is the biggest goal I would love to achieve?

A:

Once you have considered this, start to write down some small actions you could take today to take you one step closer to achieving your HUGG.

What's your Inspiration?

Setting those goals (or intentions as I also like to refer to them because when we intend to do something it makes it a *must* rather than a *should* do it) is often born from being inspired by something, but that also works the other way in that the goal you set yourself can inspire you too. I'm a fan of having a mix of HUGGs, mid-size and smaller goals, using the smaller intentions as steps to the bigger ones, creating a pathway to your ultimate vision.

Inspiration is hugely important, it's free and it's magical thinking that can be brought to life. Inspiration is not the same as motivation though. We feel inspiration internally, whilst motivation is an external driving force that influences our direction.

Your inspiration is only going to become reality if you take the action to bring those possibilities to life though.

"Everyone's dream can come true if you stick to it and work hard." Serena Williams, Tennis Champion

Inspiration is all around us, in our personal and professional lives and achieving our goals or bringing our intentions to life is always possible.

Let's PERFORM
Exercise #3
Who Inspires You?

For the next seven minutes consider three people who inspire you. What is it that they do or stand for that draws you to them? How could you bring some of these qualities into your life?

1.

2.

3.

Hope is at the Heart

If we have our goal in mind, we know it's possible to bring it to life and we are inspired to do so, how do we really get there?

This is where two other factors come into play alongside setting our goal.

Goal   our target
Agency   the motivation to reach our goal
Pathways   the route we take to reach our goal

These elements come together in American psychologist Charles Snyder's *Hope Theory* where he states: *Hope = Agency and Pathways*

Hope can be an anchor for possibility. A firm base on which to build a level of skill for peak performance and a learned behavior that can become a core element of both satisfaction and success.

With these combined elements in place not only is there hope, but a goal and possibility that lies ahead can be seen, there is a mindset of possibility (agency) and the plan of how to reach them is in place (pathways)... and that's when everything just starts to flow for us, when we reach that point where the level of challenge meets our level of skill.

... and another wonderful benefit of reaching this point? The focus on possibility creates positive emotions which breeds more positivity, making us feel happier, emotionally fitter and we flourish. Take a moment to start thinking about your mindset, goals, agency and pathways and what's possible for you and your life.

"Hope is being able to see that there is light despite all of the darkness."
Desmond Tutu, Anglican Bishop and Theologian

Let's PERFORM
Exercise #4
Free Journaling

For the next seven minutes just write...there is no need to worry about grammar, spelling or structure, just write everything that comes into your head when you think about what's possible for you. Even write down things you notice, like *"my nose is itching" or "I hear a car outside".*

Set a timer and just enjoy thinking and noticing and letting everything in your head roll onto the page, without judgement.

This exercise creates space in your mind to start to action your intentions and allows you to truly see the possibilities that lie ahead.

At the end of seven minutes read back your words. How does it feel?

Try this every time your head feels a little 'full'.

Possibility is an Art

Possibility is an art, something we can learn and develop into a superpower. Why is that the case? Because, in the words of authors Benjamin and Rosamund Zander in their book *The Art of Possibility*, *"it is all invented."* Everything is invented and when you come to understand that, you start to believe that you are surrounded by a world of possibility.

You realize there is no perfect way to do things or to be, you understand that you can do things your way for the best outcome for you and you believe there are several different pathways to make things possible. 2+2 isn't the only way to make 4.

Get Creative

Creative thinking can often make what seems impossible become possible. It helps you make that shift from *impossible* to *I'm possible.*

Creative doesn't mean being all artsy, though that is good too, it just means being open to thinking differently, open to learning and stepping away from the *that's how we've always done it* crowd.

Let's PERFORM

Exercise #5

Out of the Box

It's time to think outside of the box and open yourself up to more possibilities. This is a little brain teaser you may be familiar with that gets us thinking creatively and shows us when something feels impossible, actually, possibility is right there.

Using just four straight lines, join up all the dots without your pen leaving the paper. Simple eh?!

A Little Kindness

Opening up to possibility takes a little kindness too, not just to others but to ourselves. Self-trust and self-compassion are so important and letting go of the desire to compare ourselves to others. Comparison syndrome can have a negative impact on us. Yes, healthy competition in controlled situations is good and exciting, but in truth, the only person you have to be better than is yourself by striving to be stronger and healthier every day through kindness and growth.

Sometimes, at first it's hard to be self-aware but it's a skill we can develop through practice. Connection to the self and others takes good communication skills and good communication is reliant on both verbal and non-verbal actions.

Good listening requires empathy and kindness... two skills we are often guilty of not extending to ourselves and consequently our internal communication skills can be off kilter.

Our internal narrative has form for *mean-girling* (a form of social bullying). How often has your internal monologue told you that you *"look fat"*, *"are not good enough", or "not worthy"*? It can bully us... and we allow it to happen.

It's time to address the internal comms, put some boundaries and rules in place and connect and communicate better with ourselves... and if we don't get the answers we need, ask better questions!

Let's PERFORM

Exercise #6

Talking to a Friend

Take seven minutes to consider our self-kindness and how we communicate with ourselves and write down your thoughts.

Think of a time when a friend was really struggling with something in their life. How did you comfort them? What did you say?

Think of a time when you were really struggling with something in your life. How did you comfort yourself? What did you say?

What did you notice? Was there a difference in your verbal or non-verbal communication? If so, ask yourself why you treated the two situations so differently.

If you had treated yourself with the same kindness and compassion you extended to your friend, how would things change for you?

Connection

Connection is not only important in terms of realizing possibilities in your life, it's also a great asset for your wellness. Often, a sense of disconnection is what fuels low moods and even depression.

Connection is a superpower and connecting to our visions is essential for bringing goals and possibilities to life. Visualizing goals or intentions doesn't just mean thinking about them, it means engaging with them utilizing all your senses and then attaching an emotion to them. How does that vision make you feel?

Strive not just for the goal itself but the feeling the emotion attached to it gives you.

To effectively connect with our visions and in order to believe they are possible our priority has to be to connect with ourself and this takes a level of self-awareness, meaning you have to be able to look inwards and assess how you think and feel both emotionally and physically.

First connect with yourself and then connect with others to help realize your dreams and intentions; build your team. We don't have to do this alone. That kind of thinking can lead to burnout and negatively impact our emotional fitness. Be a contribution, a part of the process and this will lead to greater possibilities and satisfaction and ultimately happiness and flourishing.

Who is in your team and can be part of your support crew to help you achieve your goals, perform at your best and live your best life?

Write down their names and welcome them into your inner circle of trust and possibility.

"I define connection as the energy that exists between people when they feel seen, heard, and valued; when they can give and receive without judgement; and when they derive sustenance and strength from the relationship."

Dr. Brené Brown, researcher, author & speaker

Affirmations

Another way to connect and communicate with ourselves in order to bring our possibilities to life is through affirmations.

Affirmations are positive statements which we can repeat in order to affirm possibilities, desires and intentions and help to overcome negative and self-sabotaging thoughts.

Never forget that the stories we tell our brains our brains believe, so if we consistently affirm positive statements our brain will wire itself to believe them.

Affirmations can help us PERFORM better by increasing confidence, calming nervous thoughts and making what we think is possible become a reality. Research also indicates that affirmations can help manage stress, so they have a positive impact on our emotional fitness levels.

Affirmations aren't just magical thinking; they are a tool that can help develop positive thinking and emotions in order for us to manifest our biggest goals, dreams and desires.

Once we believe something is possible we want to manifest it into existence and that means aligning our thoughts with our own energy and the actions we take. These three combined factors can make anything possible.

Let's PERFORM
Exercise #7
Positive Affirmation List

For seven minutes write down a list of positive affirmations. Start each sentence with "I am..."

If you want you can break them down into different categories such as personal, professional, health, or physical. For example:

"I am happy"

"I am healthy"

"I am creative"

"I am safe"

"I am taking the action to be successful"

"I am a valuable contribution to my team"

"I am worthy"

"I am curious"

Once you have written them down, read them back to yourself. How does it make you feel?

Any time you need a boost in self-confidence or self-compassion, come back to this list and read it to yourself, or repeat the exercise writing down positive affirmation statements starting with "I am."

It's so important to remember you are energy and everything around you is energy and we need to work to keep our energetic vibration high.

What this means is we are all living energy fields as our bodies are made up of energy-producing particles, all of which are constantly moving. Everyone and everything in the universe is vibrating and creating energy and the higher and more we vibrate the higher the energy.

According to researcher, psychiatrist and teacher Dr. David. R. Hawkins and his Map of Consciousness and diagram of vibrational states, the level our energy vibrates at, can range from shame to enlightenment and by implementing exercises and tools consistently, such as those in this book, you will not only raise your vibrational and energy levels, you can protect your mental health, become emotionally fitter, be more resilient and flourish and you will manifest into your life everything you believe is truly possible.

You will live an abundant life full of happiness, wealth and good health.

"Decide what you want to be, do and have. Think the thoughts of it, emit the frequency and your vision will become your life."
Rhonda Byrne, author of *'The Secret'*

Anything is possible and when we realize that, when we align our energy with our thoughts and we take the consistent action to make our visions a reality, we can really start to PERFORM. What is possible for you?

ENJOYMENT

The way to... Find Joy!

Joy... the central column of the word *enjoyment* and something many people spend a lifetime seeking, thinking that joy and happiness will be presented to them on a silver platter when they achieve something or reach a certain state of fulfilment... this is not how it should be.

Enjoyment, often referred to as joy, fun, happiness or luxury, is the process of taking pleasure in something. It's not something we should be striving for, but a daily tool we should be utilizing to perform at our best. *Enjoyment* is essential for flourishing, for emotional fitness and to be mentally healthier. *Enjoyment* does not need a permission slip and you should never be ashamed to do what you love and love what you do. When you live life on this premise, there is a whole world of possibility open to you.

"Enjoy the journey, enjoy every moment, and quit worrying about winning and losing."
Matt Biondi – three time Olympic champion swimmer

Why is Enjoyment Important?

It's a good question really... why is it important to experience enjoyment? Well, apart from anything it makes us feel good, boosting those positive emotions and helping us to be emotionally fitter and mentally healthier. Enjoyment helps us flourish.

If we aren't enjoying something we engage in, it can affect our mood, lead to negative feelings, frustration, more stress and ultimately affect our standard of performance and our relationships.

There is a belief that one should *suffer for their art,* but really there is no reason why we can't be happy in what we do... the *loving what we do and doing what we love* mindset. That is literally the ethos my business is built on!

In everything that we do there may be some pain, some discomfort, but there are no laws to say we cannot bring enjoyment to the party... Enjoyment is quite a good friend and guest to have at any party!

Let's PERFORM
Exercise #1
Design a Beautiful Day

Take seven minutes to design a beautiful day. What does a *beautiful day* mean to you? What do you love to do or haven't had chance to do recently?

If time and logistics weren't an issue, how would you spend your time and who with?

Write down your thoughts and add in details such as who you are with, what you see, what you eat...

How does this *beautiful day* make you feel?

What's stopping this *beautiful day* from becoming a reality?

What are your Strengths?

There are some things that we are really good at. That could be anything from how you listen to friends in need to your unicycling skills! We also have things that aren't quite in our wheelhouse... like running (definitely not on my strengths list!) or sticking to a schedule or plan.

Can you identify your strengths?

You'd be amazed at how many people are actually unaware of their strengths. However, if we were aware and we worked with our strengths on a regular basis in all that we do, we would enjoy our activities far more.

Research suggests that people who make greater use of their strengths develop a greater level of wellness. It was also said that we gain more when we build on our talents, as opposed to when we make an effort to improve our weaknesses.

What exactly is a strength?

A strength contributes to our character and helps to regulate our emotional fitness and mental health. It can help us be balanced and have a good relationship with ourself and others. It can both boost and compromise our character, making us both strong, but also vulnerable.

A strength can be both internally or externally motivated; we can engage in the strength because either we personally enjoy the activity – it is an intrinsic motivation - or we want to earn an external reward from the activity – it is an extrinsic motivation.

Often the word *strength* is less associated with our emotions than the physical strength of someone – think *strong man* in a circus or *The World's Strongest Man*.

When we are not *strong* at something it is often referred to as a weakness, but we tend to perceive weakness as negative. However just because we are not good at something doesn't mean we are necessarily weak at it... it could be that we just haven't developed that strength. If we wanted to remove the negative connotation of a weakness we could refer to our strengths as *tonic* and *phasic*.

This means that our *tonic strengths* are those things we are particularly strong at whilst our *phasic strengths* are the strengths we use less.

There is also a danger that a strength we use too far could become a so-called weakness, for example, being overly kind could lead you to be taken advantage of.

"Try to look at your weakness and convert it into your strength. That's success."
Hilary Hinton 'Zig' Ziglar, author and speaker

A strength can and should be consistently worked on and developed for the benefit of peak performance, health and wellness as the development of a strength brings resilience.

So, I revert to my previous question... *can you identify your strengths?*

Don't worry if you can't, you are not alone, but let's use our next exercise to help you identify your tonic and phasic strengths so you can work with your strengths and not against them.

Identifying your strengths will help you flourish, increase your happiness and wellness and help you perform at your best.

If you perform with a team (be that workplace, sport, music or any type of team) this can also be very effective as you can get your whole team to work with their strengths for increased productivity, performance and the development of a mentally healthy culture.

Let's PERFORM

Exercise #2

Identify your Strengths

An effective way to identify your strengths is by using a positive psychology based questionnaire such as the VIA Institute on Character's *Character Strengths Survey.* Head to the website at www.viacharacter.org and take the free survey. The questionnaire lists 24 strengths which are divided between six virtues:

Wisdom (creativity, curiosity, judgment, love of learning, perspective); **Courage** (bravery, honesty, perseverance, zest); **Humanity** (kindness, love, social intelligence); **Justice** (fairness, leadership, teamwork); **Temperance** (forgiveness, humility, prudence, self-regulation); **Transcendence** (appreciation of beauty and excellence, gratitude, hope, humor, spirituality).

On completion you will receive an ordered list of your strengths. Start to focus on your top five, aligning your personal and professional life with utilizing these tonic strengths on a daily basis and see how it affects your satisfaction and enjoyment of life.

It's All in the Preparation

"Proper preparation prevents poor performance."
James Baker, former US Secretary of State

Familiar with those 5 Ps? Or maybe the military motto of *proper planning and preparation prevents p*ss poor performance* is more on your radar?

Either way, being as prepared as possible for a situation is going to give you a lot more enjoyable performance and outcome.

Preparation means planning your action, organizing your resources and doing the work to not just make sure you can perform, but doing the work to make sure things in your control can't go wrong.

There will always be elements of your personal, professional or social life that will be beyond your control - bad, annoying and disappointing things happen – but by preparing ourselves for what is within our control we not only increase the likelihood of our enjoyment, we also boost our self-confidence and self-esteem.

A huge and essential part of preparation is your mindset. How you feel about and approach a situation not only influences your mood and enjoyment level, it also dictates your level of performance.

Think negatively and your brain believes this is the state of mind you want to achieve; think positively and your brain will believe you.

"We are shaped by our thoughts; we become what we think. When the mind is pure, joy follows like a shadow that never leaves."
Buddha

Whatever performance you are preparing for, be it at work, sporting event, on stage, solo or with a team, or just in everyday life, there are certain things we can do to prepare... and the most important thing is to address your mindset.

Let's PERFORM
Exercise #3
Best Possible Future

Spend seven minutes considering an upcoming situation or event which requires you to perform with confidence and which you want to enjoy.

Write down what this scenario looks like if everything goes completely to plan for you. What does this best possible future look like? Don't think about potential issues or what could go wrong, purely focus on what is good and right and note down what it looks like, what it feels like and how you respond.

Not only does this exercise help you to visualize the situation in full detail, it gives us a positive state of mind to continue with and changes our mindset to a positive outlook for maximum success and enjoyment.

What's the Challenge?

Once we have identified situations or events we need to prepare for and are viewing them with a positive mindset, it is then important to also identify factors which could pose a threat and hijack our enjoyment.

We need challenges in our life, they help us learn, grow and find freedom and in order to truly enjoy challenges that face us we need to have an awareness of possible threats and potential pitfalls on our pathway to perform. Once analyzed we need to turn these challenges into opportunities, reframing our thoughts in-line with our positive mindset.

A positive mindset doesn't mean that we believe everything is going to be OK, rather it means that whatever challenge we face we know we will be OK. Positivity is not about being optimistic or pessimistic, it is being realistic, knowing that for true enjoyment we need a combination of possibility and action.

"A pessimist sees the difficulty in every opportunity; an optimist sees the opportunity in every difficulty." Winston Churchill, former UK Prime Minister

Let's PERFORM
Exercise #4
From Challenge to Strategy

Take seven minutes to consider the scenario you wrote about in Exercise #3.

Now you have a positive mindset about this scenario, write down what challenges you face in this situation.

Write down one potential challenge and then three ways you could meet this challenge, including details of what action you can take and who can help you.

The one challenge is...

I can meet this challenge by:

1.

2.

3.

Will implementing these strategies help you enjoy this challenge?

Finding your Flow

When our skill level (which we have enhanced by identifying and working with our strengths) matches the challenge level that we face, we are on schedule for maximum enjoyment of any event or performance.

This sweet spot is called *Flow* or perhaps you have heard it as being *in the zone.* Whatever terminology you use, it's that point in our actions where time passes quickly and things feel easy because we are enjoying and mastering the activity. This *Flow state* which was defined by the esteemed positive psychologist Mihaly Csikszentmihalyi also allows for an enhancement of managing anxiety.

When strengths have been identified it becomes easier to match skill level to challenge in order to achieve Flow. A person becomes fully immersed in their activity with a feeling of energy and enjoyment in the process of the activity, hence the importance of *Enjoyment* as a core element of the PERFORM framework to increase wellness to protect mental health.

A Flow state is not just limited to creatives, performers and sportspeople though; we can experience Flow in every day life. Ever been on that car journey that went really quickly and you don't quite remember it all or experienced something so pleasurable that you were sad when it was over because it felt like it finished too quickly? They are real life examples of a non-performance Flow state.

You may have also had situations where an activity or performance you were taking part in just felt really comfortable and easy and that gave you a huge sense of satisfaction and enjoyment. This is Flow.

Flow is completely achievable when we match our skill level and the level of challenge, which is why preparation and knowing your strengths are so important and indicative of achieving Flow.

Let's PERFORM

Exercise #5

From Fear to Flow

Take seven minutes to consider two different scenarios.

1.A time when you totally enjoyed an activity or performance which meant time passed really quickly.

2.A time when an activity or performance felt difficult and dragged on.

What was different about these two scenarios?

- What was your mindset prior to the events?

- How did you prepare for both events?

- Did you utilize your tonic strengths for both?

- Who else was involved in both events?

- What story did you tell yourself before and after each event?

Write down anything you notice which could help you achieve a Flow state in the future and perform at your best.

Reaching the Peak

Experiencing a Flow state often means we are performing at our best and peak performance is a state we should strive for in all that we do, whether in our personal or professional lives. The term peak performance means an outstanding performance which is given under regular conditions, hinting that it is something everyone can experience and reap the benefits from.

We should want to be the best we can be at our jobs, as a parent, friend, child or sibling and striving for peak performance and performing at our best with optimum satisfaction helps us truly enjoy activities and increase our emotional fitness. Conversely, being emotionally fit and flourishing also promotes peak performance, so whichever way you look at it, striving to perform at your best is healthy for you.

Peak performance means different things to different people and can be related to individuals or groups. Peak or high-performance relates to those individuals, teams, organisations or groups that are highly focused on their goals and consequently achieve superior results. They not only outperform others but they also outperform expectations for enjoyment and reward.

They also work within a high-performance culture, designed to make them as effective as possible at identifying and reaching goals.

Peak performance is not just results focused though, it is about performing at your best and exceeding your own expectations and is internally motivated and driven. It is about constant analysis to change to be your best; be satisfied and feel enjoyment and by focusing on these elements, the reward of results will follow. Peak performance is a mindset.

"If you focus on results you will never change.
If you focus on change you will get results."
Jack Dixon, Welsh Rugby Union player

Let's PERFORM
Exercise #6
Make a Change

For seven minutes think about a time that relied on you performing at your best.

- Did you perform at your best on that occasion?
- What made it so good?
- If you didn't perform at your best on that occasion what stopped your peak performance opportunity?
- What could you change in your preparation, mindset or approach next time to promote consistent high-performance?

Time for a Boost!

The joy of performing at your best is that it makes us feel good. It boosts our mood and our confidence which consequently increases our emotional fitness, make us mentally healthier and encourages us to keep undertaking the activities at our highest level.

There is a danger that we could become complacent that the feel-good sensation will always be experienced when we undertake the activities that led us to peak performance, but if we take time to understand and appreciate that performing at our best and experiencing a Flow state take continued mastery of our mindset and skills, we stand ourself in good stead for enjoyment, satisfaction and success.

The extra bonus of the boost in mood and self-confidence from peak performance is that it encourages us to continue to do the work and thus a cycle of positive emotions occurs.

When we experience positive emotions and feelings we are more likely to do the work to breed more positive emotions and we enter into a positive upwards spiral, named the *Broaden and Build Theory* by psychologist Barbara Fredrickson.

The other thing that brings us enjoyment in all that we have to do is...having fun!

We need to play more, be more childlike, put our worries and inhibitions to one side and make our lives, work, teams and environments more fun. Even the most serious and important work can have a dusting of the *'light and fluffy'* about it and creating a culture of *play* is both healthy and inspiring.

Life is hard, work is hard, difficult things will always happen, but that doesn't mean we can't find a way to enjoy everything we do by implementing fun and laughter into our worlds... and we must.

"Live and work but do not forget to play, to have fun in life and really enjoy it."
Eileen Caddy, founder of Findhorn Foundation

Let's PERFORM
Exercise #7
Three Funny Things

You may be familiar with the gratitude exercise *Three Things* which asks you to write down three things that happened during the day that you are grateful for. It's a great exercise to do just before bedtime because the time we spend reflecting on those events and feelings of gratitude we feel boost our positive emotions and, if timed just before we sleep, can mean we also wake the next morning with a heightened mood.

Here is a little twist to the exercise. Write down three things that you found fun or funny today.

1.

2.

3.

How easy or hard was that? If it was easy you can reflect on those fun or funny things to give yourself an instant mood boost. If you found it a little harder, take it as a sign to seek out more fun in your days and repeat the exercise daily.

Love what you do and do what you love...

Doing the things we love, using the skills we are good at and feeling the emotional and physical benefits in our mood and health helps us to enjoy life, be more motivated, inspired, satisfied and successful.

This enjoyment is open to us all and is a consequence of our awareness of our strengths and challenges and the commitment to taking regular, consistent action to perform at our best.

When we start to focus on enjoyment and dismiss the belief that success equals suffering, not only do we enjoy life more, but we really start to PERFORM.

I hope you enjoyed this section. Now go and have fun!

RESILIENCE

the way to... Build Resilience

"Do not judge me by my success, judge me by how many times I fell down and got back up again."

Nelson Mandela, anti-Apartheid activist and politician

Building resilience is a fundamental part of living a flourishing life. It is a key to being emotional fitter and by building resilience and embracing positive emotions we build an upward spiral towards happiness and thriving, not just surviving.

Being happy is not just about experiencing all the good things in life, it's equally about making sure we have good resilience skills in order to manage the difficult and stressful experiences that come along... because we will all face something difficult and uncomfortable that we have to navigate.

According to the Merriam-Webster dictionary, resilience is *the ability to easily adjust to misfortune or change.* It's often been explained as an ability to *bounce back,* but the issue with this definition is that it implies you revert back to your previous state, when in fact you could become stronger or revert to a different form when your grit has been tested.

When we talk about recovery from any mental health issue or difficult situation, that recovery is not always linear or mean returning to that cookie-cutter version of yourself. It could be a more flourishing version or a managed recovery; be that with therapies or medications.

The same is true of resilience – it is not always *bouncing back* to that previous version, it's very possible a much wiser version awaits you.

Resilience (or mental strength as it's sometimes referred to) is strongly connected with hope, and acts as a protective factor for your mental health. That's why it's such an important part of the PERFORM framework, which is designed to boost emotional fitness, promote wellness and protect mental health.

Let's PERFORM

Exercise #1

Resilience Quiz

This quiz is adapted from the *Resilience Advantage* by Al Siebert PhD, founder of The Resiliency Center in Portland, Oregon.

Rate yourself from 1 to 5 on the following: (1 = very little, 5 = very strong)

- In a crisis or chaotic situation, I calm myself and focus on taking useful actions.

- I'm usually optimistic. I see difficulties as temporary and expect to overcome them.

- I can tolerate high levels of ambiguity and uncertainty about situations.

- I adapt quickly to new developments. I'm good at bouncing back from difficulties.

- I'm playful. I find the humour in rough situations, and can laugh at myself.

- I'm able to recover emotionally from losses and setbacks.

- I have friends I can talk with. I can express my feelings to others and ask for help.

- Feelings of anger, loss and discouragement don't last long.

- I feel self-confident, appreciate myself, and have a healthy concept of who I am.

- I'm curious. I ask questions. I want to know how things work. I like to try new ways of doing things.

- I learn valuable lessons from my experiences and from the experiences of others.

- I'm good at solving problems. I can use analytical logic, be creative, or use practical common sense.

- I'm good at making things work well. I'm often asked to lead groups and projects.

- I'm always myself, but I've noticed that I'm different in different situations.

- I prefer to work without a written job description. I'm more effective when I'm free to do what I think is best in each situation.

- I "read" people well and trust my intuition.

- I'm a good listener. I have good empathy skills.

- I'm non-judgmental about others and adapt to people's different personality styles.

- I've been made stronger and better by difficult experiences.

- I've converted misfortune into good luck and found benefits in bad experiences.

_____ Total

Resiliency Quiz Scoring

80 or higher: Highly Resilient -
you thrive under pressure

65-80: Good Resilience –
you recover well from most challenges

50-65: Some Resilience –
you have some resiliency skills

40-50: Not Much Resilience –
you may have trouble handling pressure

40 or under: Low Resilience –
you may feel hopeless or helpless at times

The Higher the Hope...

"I can be changed by what happens to me, but I refuse to be reduced by it."
Maya Angelou, American writer &
civil rights activist

Research suggests that people with higher levels of hope are more resilient. They may also experience less anxiety and depression and experience more positive outcomes in their personal and professional activities.

Higher-hope people are also more inclined to adapt when things go wrong, by developing better coping strategies than lower-hope people. There is also a symmetry between hope levels and self-confidence and those with a higher level of self-awareness and self-care will likely not only have more hope, but more resilience too.

Furthermore, those with low levels of hope are also likely to lack self-confidence which means they may not experience *Flow* as they are less likely to set goals.

Using Hope as an Anchor

One way of considering hope and resilience is that hopeful people who possess the skill of positive thinking have a good and realistic sense of what's possible for them and when we pair resilience with this sense of hope and possibility it becomes pivotal in how someone responds to stress and difficult situations.

Where possibility is hopeful thinking, resilience is action and, hope plus action equals resilience and emotional fitness.

Taking action by implementing positive psychology based activities into our lives and wellness toolkit, plus having a hopeful mindset could build resilience and emotional fitness to protect mental health.

Similar to positive emotions, resilience is self-perpetuating. The more you have, the more you build.

Resiliency re-directs our mind in moments of adversity, helping us to return to form.

Let's PERFORM

Exercise #2

Three Good Things

Spend seven minutes doing this activity to build positive emotions. The more positive emotions we have, the more we build and this in turn helps to build resilience.

•   End your day by considering three good things that happened today. Write them down.

•   Reflect on the experiences noting how they made you feel in that moment and ask yourself what was the best thing about the experience.

By reflecting on our experiences it expands our capacity for positive emotions, gratitude and helps us become more emotionally attuned to ourselves, all of which has an impact on our resilience.

Time for Reflection

Now we've looked at the good things in your day, take a moment to look at what you've experienced already in your life. If you're reading this now then that means you've likely got through some hard stuff so you already have some resiliency skills; you just may not be utilizing them to the max. Appreciate that and be grateful for all you've achieved. You have literally survived 100% of your days on earth so far!

Once you look back at things you can change the narrative going forwards; in effect you can choose not only how to live your life, but choose your mindset and how you respond and act to situations without reacting in the heat of the moment. Reflecting back is very important for learning and building resilience, however, we don't want to stay stuck in the past.

You can face your fears, release regrets, cultivate forgiveness of yourself and others you feel may have done wrong to you and you can learn the lessons to help you develop your strength and resilience.

"Only those who dare to fail greatly, can ever achieve greatly."
Robert F. Kennedy, American lawyer
and politician

When we take a moment to reflect we can start to notice patterns in our life; patterns in the way we deal with positive or negative events. We may even notice and appreciate breakthroughs – a moment in time when everything changed for you. A moment when impossible becomes *I'm possible*.

There are three parts to a breakthrough. State, story and strategy. Our state affects our story which dictates our strategy.

Our life is not always chaotic, it is just our patterns at play and sometimes we need to have courage to recognize old patterns that don't serve us and create new ones. Sometimes we may be scared to do this, but we need to do it anyway. That's building resilience.

Let's PERFORM
Exercise #3
Acknowledge your Breakthrough

Take seven minutes to acknowledge your breakthrough.

1. What was your breakthrough? What was something you struggled with for a long time but finally broke through?

2. What was the moment that changed it all? What made this change a *MUST* for you and not just *I should change?*

3. What made it possible for that change to last? Perhaps a new belief or strategy?

How does it feel recognizing your old patterns and creating new ones for more resilience and happiness?

"Fall seven times, stand up eight."
Japanese proverb

Take Time Out

Taking time out from the busy world, both emotionally and physically, is a good thing. We can't just keep doing things out of habit or impulse as this is not sustainable for emotional fitness. It is OK, great and even essential to do nothing sometimes; we don't always have to be striving forwards. Being mindful of what's going on right now and slowing down is good for your mind, body and spirit.

When we do nothing it's also the time when our body and mind can absorb everything they have learned. A good example of this is a *Savasana* at the end of a yoga practice. You know, the moment at the end of the workout when you get to lie down on your back doing nothing – the bit everyone loves! One of the main purposes of the Savasana is to allow the body the time to absorb the full effects of the workout.

Let's PERFORM
Exercise #4
Permission to do Nothing

It's time for seven minutes of nothing, yes you heard right, nothing!

Lie flat on your back for seven minutes. Allow thoughts to come into your head then send them on their way again. You can imagine them floating off on a cloud.

This seven minutes is your permission to do nothing, to allow your mind and body the opportunity and time to absorb what they have learned both physically and emotionally.

How does it feel after seven minutes?

Reflection done, time out taken, now it's time to focus on how you have got through the tough things so far and how you can develop those skills. If things aren't always working for you, taking a break can really help and don't be afraid to make changes and change patterns.

Create a Little Change

"We are not a product of what has happened to us in the past. We have the power of choice."
Stephen Covey, educator and author

Creating and being creative are important for resilience as it's our capacity to learn, change and grow that gives us options in how to handle situations.

You have the means to create yourself, your life, what and how you do things and you shouldn't be shy of *rebranding* yourself at any time.

Your story is based on your identity and your identity does, and needs to, change as you learn and grow.

Create a plan of what you want, what you need and how you can implement that and combined with an element of letting things *be* and *happen*, you can really bump up your resilience levels.

Remember, life happens *for you* and not *to you.* No matter how hard a situation seems or how big an obstacle feels, there is a lesson that awaits you and building your resilience will make you more open to receiving these lessons.

When we feel stuck and like our resiliency skills are lacking, it feels like we aren't capable of change, but that is just not true.

This is simply the story we have told ourselves and what we consequently believe. A belief is something we know for certain, so what we believe dictates our outcomes.

I've already mentioned the three stages of a breakthrough; state, story and strategy. Let's think about how we can get creative with our story to change our beliefs and be more resilient.

Let's PERFORM

Exercise #5

Create your Story

Try this thoughtful exercises for seven minutes.

• What is a story you are telling yourself? Think of a situation that feels difficult to navigate.

• What is your role in this story?

• What is your best future story for this situation?

• What emotions can you attach to that best future? How do you want to feel?

Now think of one small action you can take NOW to create your new story.

Get Moving

"Our greatest weakness lies in giving up. The most certain way to succeed is always to try just one more time." Thomas Edison, inventor

With your armory of developed skills, it's time to move. Literal physical movement will help to give your mind clarity, improve your wellness and mental and physical health. The best thing about moving is, by changing our physiological state, we actually change our emotional state. We can change our mood by moving our body.

We are all energy, everything around us is energy and if we want to feel stronger or more resilient then we need to raise our energetic vibration... and that comes from moving. Now, when we think about this concept of energy intellectually it may not make sense or mean much, but when we feel it physically and our energy is raised we can feel how it affects us mentally. Raising our energy gives us more mental clarity and more mental clarity means more resilience. Higher energy also equals more happiness.

Building resilience requires moving in a different way, aside from changing our physiology. It also means moving forwards with our life. Knowing that whatever difficult situation we have to face, there is a pathway forwards and our resilience level dictates how effectively and smoothly we make that move.

There is no speed guidance for this forward momentum, as long as the direction is forwards, you do you and move at your own speed to achieve the satisfaction that you need and want.

Never forget this is your life on your terms. Work on your resilience and you can navigate life and all its ups and downs with a little more confidence and ease.

Let's PERFORM
Exercise #6
Walk the Dog

Don't worry if you don't actually have a dog. This is just the name for a quick seven minute activity I want you to implement into your day when you feel you need to change your state, raise your mood, build your resilience and get creative in your mind and thoughts.

• Take a walk outside for seven minutes. Just a quick walk round the block. No music, audiobooks, podcasts or tech, just a quick stretch of the legs... and take the dog if you have one! (or create an imaginary one!).

The combination of movement, fresh air and nature is powerful and will bring you some mental clarity and change your physical and mental state, thus meaning filling your resilience capacity.

"Grief and resilience live together."
Michelle Obama, former FLOTUS

One thing is very certain in our lives and that is that our resilience levels will be tested. Whether its stress at work, family dynamics, parenting, financial, job or housing issues, global events and situations, mental or physical health issues or the loss of someone or something and navigating grief, hard things will happen and it's not enough to think *I'll deal with it when it happens.* We need to function from a more protective narrative and build our resiliency resources so when something difficult happens, which it will, we have the capacity to not just survive it but to thrive from it and grow. That's why building in these activities into your consistent daily life is so important.

… and if everything else just feels too hard, we can always come back to our breath to ground ourselves.

Let's PERFORM
Exercise #7
Affirmation Breathing

Affirmations are powerful. As soon as we add *I am* to the start of a sentence we believe what we say next and as we have already established our beliefs are something we know for certain.

In moments where we need our resilience most, there is one exercise we can always come back to and that is breathing. Breathing exercises are the most fundamental of all resources, and they are free. They de-escalate our heart rate and allow our bodies to function at their best.

In this final activity we combine these two resources for one powerful exercise to build resilience.

Pop a timer on and try this exercise for the next seven minutes. If you are capable try these exercises breathing through your nose.

Say these affirmations internally to the self and repeat this box breathing exercise.

Breathe in for 4 beats - Affirmation: "I can overcome my obstacles."

Hold for 4 beats - Affirmation: "I am resilient."

Breathe out for 4 beats - Affirmation: "I am strong."

Hold for 4 beats - Affirmation: "I am empowered."

How do you feel? Make a note of the emotions and sensations that came up for you.

"Rock bottom became the solid foundation on which I built my life."

J. K. Rowling, author

Emotional Fitness is not about the absence of illness. It is increasing resources which enhance wellness for health, building hope and resilience and my hope for you is that by reading this book you have not only learned a few quick and simple ways to be more resilient, you have further developed your wellness toolkit to be emotionally fitter and flourish.

I hope this section was an enjoyable read.

FOCUS

the way to... Focus

"It is during our darkest moments that we must focus to see the light." Aristotle Onassis, Greek Argentinian shipping magnate

It is said that depression is often triggered when we are thinking about things in the past and anxiety is triggered when we are worrying about things in the future. Our minds spend a lot of time thinking about what's been or what's coming and this means we forget to appreciate the present moment.

Consider this a moment.

How do you feel right now?

What can you see, feel, hear, taste and smell?

By engaging all your senses you become mindful of the *now* and this increases your focus, allowing you to increase your energy level to perform at your best.

When we focus on the activity we are engaging in and the challenge meets the level of enjoyment we enter what is termed as a state of *Flow.*

According to the psychologist who developed *Flow Theory*, Mihaly Csikszentmihalyi, Flow is: *"a state in which people are so involved in an activity that nothing else seems to matter."*

This state of Flow allows for great focus, which in turn keeps the mind sharp and mentally fit, meaning that our focus not only impacts our levels of success, but our levels of satisfaction and our emotional fitness, and being emotionally fitter means we are protecting our mental health.

Let's take a moment straight away to focus our mind and become really aware of the present moment, how we feel in our mind and body and create a *proneness for Flow.* In other words, get the stage set and ourselves prepared to optimize our focus to perform at our best.

Let's PERFORM
Exercise #1
Body Scan

Read this exercise through first and then set aside seven minutes to enjoy this body scan meditation. Read through the instructions a few times and then try it yourself.

• Sit or lie down, close your eyes, and take a few moments to relax.

• Once you're relaxed, take a moment to check your posture. Make sure you are comfortable and that your spine is in proper alignment. Place your hands on your lap or by your side, palms upwards. Make sure your neck and body is relaxed, including all the muscles in your face.

- With your eyes closed, focus on the sensations throughout your entire body. Simply observe the way your body feels. Focus the mind on those sensations.

- Direct your mind to the crown of your head. Notice the sensations there. Focus on the way the crown of your head feels.

- Now gradually begin to move your focus down your body, through your face.

- Continue to pass your consciousness down your neck, your shoulders, your arms, all the way to your fingers. Then proceed back up your arms to your shoulders, and then down to your feet and toes. Meditate on each part of the body before moving on.

- Once you've reached your toes, reverse the procedure until you are once again focusing on the crown of your head.

- Now take a moment to feel the sensations throughout your entire body. Take a few moments to relax before returning to normal.

- Continue to tune in to your body throughout the day in order to stay mindful.

Be Present!

"Realize deeply that the present moment is all you ever have. Make the Now the primary focus of your life." Eckhart Tolle, author and spiritual teacher

Individuals are fully absorbed in the present moment when they experience Flow and a key skill for being present and developing a proneness for Flow is Focus.

Mindfulness is a focus technique that arises from thinking about the present moment without judgement and by having a more mindful, focused and accepting manner, we can potentially create conditions that foster Flow, which may be useful for helping to alleviate anxious feelings by reducing self-loathing and criticism.

There are some misconceptions about mindfulness, mainly that is about sitting around meditating, having zero thoughts and chanting strange noises, but this really isn't the case.

Being mindful simply means being more aware and taking notice of all your senses and environment.

Let's PERFORM

Exercise #2

5-4-3-2-1-Grounded

Being mindful means engaging with all your senses and this focus technique called *Grounding* is perfect for bringing yourself into the present moment because it allows you to focus on all your senses right now.

Take a seven minute break and try this exercise.

Sit comfortably and take a few deep breaths, relaxing your shoulders.

- Consider 5 things you can see right now.
- Consider 4 things you can touch right now.
- Consider 3 things you can hear right now
- Consider 2 things you can smell right now.
- Consider 1 thing you taste right now.

This exercise not only brings you into the present moment, it also reduces nerves and anxious feelings.

How do you feel right now?

Get Motivated!

"I don't care too much what happened in the past. I prefer on what is coming next and I am really looking forward to it. "
Sebastian Vettel, 4 times F1 racing world champion

Often there is confusion between inspiration, motivation and influence. Quite simply, inspiration is something you feel from within, motivation is an external element or factor that gets you going and influence is what makes you go in a particular direction.

But, in order to be motivated we also need to have a big dose of self-determination. Why? Because by being self-determined this can help us to assert personal control over our choices in life.

Self-determination also leads to better self-regulation - meaning we are more likely to take responsibility for what we do and don't do in our lives.

Let's PERFORM
Exercise #3
Time to Journal

Utilizing this journalling exercise takes an element of self-determination and self-regulation and when you utilize these questions in a consistent way you will feel more motivated and focused. You will also become emotionally fitter, have a greater level of wellness and be mentally healthier. So what are you waiting for? Let's PERFORM... Take seven minutes to answer these questions and write down your responses.

- What is one big thing you want to achieve this week?

- What are three smaller things to achieve?

- How will you feel when you achieve these things?

What's your Motivation?

"That's been one of my mantras – focus and simplicity. Simple can be harder than complex. You have to work hard to get your thinking clean to make it simple. But it's worth it in the end because once you get there, you can move mountains."

Steve Jobs, American entrepreneur

Motivation can be described as either *wanting* or *needing* and when we both need and want to change that's when we can get laser-focused on the *how* we change.

When we spend too long on the *how* we should change or achieve something, we get caught up in technical and logistical side of *how* and that means all the while we are thinking *how,* is less time we are taking action and moving towards our goal.

We need to focus more on the *why* we want to change or achieve a goal and the *what* we want to feel as we do it. Tuning ourselves into our state of mind, and indeed changing our state of mind, will likely lead us to a quicker, more effective and sustainable change.

But here's a question.

What's motivating you? Are you being driven from within or being externally fueled? This is what we refer to as *intrinsic* or *extrinsic* motivation.

Intrinsic motivation is more internal. It's when we do something because we really enjoy it, whereas *extrinsic* motivation is driven by external reward.

For example, if I entered a running race (really never likely to happen but go with me on this!) and I entered because I loved running, wanted to get better and I wanted to connect with other like-minded runners, this would be an *intrinsic* motivation.

However, if I entered the race purely because I wanted to win, be awarded a medal and be hailed the champion, this would be more *extrinsic;* I'm more motivated by the material reward than the fact I enjoy running.

There is nothing wrong with *extrinsic* motivation, it can motivate us to be hyper-focused and be highly successful, but if you're looking for more satisfaction than success, *intrinsic* motivation is where the money is at.

This is possibly a good time to mention balance. We get told to bring more balance into our lives but is that really possible? Does balance really even exist? The answer is actually more likely to be *no.* There is no such thing as balance. We can't balance all the things that we need to focus on; something has to give. So forget balance and work on integrating or blending your life and work and focus on your priorities.

We need to keep things simple; know it's OK to not prioritise some tasks and let them just be. For example, maybe your life is so full of your career and children – those are your priorities at the moment – so worrying about wearing the latest fashion trends is not high on your focus radar. That's OK. Drop thinking about your fashion choices from your list as a *not a priority now* and allow yourself permission not to prioritise it and don't feel guilty for that. Making that choice frees your mind and enhances your focus on things that actually are your priority.

We can't, nor should, do *ALL* the things. We absolutely can do anything, but we can't do everything, so cut yourself some slack... and if you're trying to do things perfectly then you're just setting yourself up for failure because perfect does not exist.

Keep your motivation simple and your focus will be supercharged, leading you to attain your goals and experience the very best of your life and perform at your best.

Let's PERFORM
Exercise #4
Design a Beautiful Day

Who doesn't love a beautiful day? This exercise allows you to create a wonderful day full of positivity and hope. Set aside seven minutes to do the following:

- Think about what a beautiful day would look like to you. What do you enjoy doing, who with and where?
- In your mind (or write down) design a beautiful day (24 hours) that would be possible for you to undertake in the next few weeks.
- Where will you go? What will you do? What will you eat? How will it feel? Identify every moment in as much detail as possible.

How does this feel? Schedule that day into your diary as a non-negotiable event. Go and live it and enjoy!

Get Goal Focused

"The game has its ups and downs, but you can never lose focus of your individual goals and you can't let yourself be beat because of lack of effort."
Michael Jordan, former pro basketball player

Goals give us our benchmark of what we are aiming for and they are important in order to give ourselves something to focus on. We can have big goals, little goals and everything in between goals. They can be realistic and achievable and they can be our wildest dreams which, with the right strategy and action, can also be achievable. Authors Andy Cope and Andy Whittaker refer to huge life changing goals as HUGGs in their book *The Art of Being Brilliant.*

There is no doubting goals are good but I also want to give you another perspective, and that is instead of setting goals, set intentions.

Every 1st of January millions of people set new year's resolutions and how many have given up within the month? I'll go to the gym, I'll give up alcohol or smoking, or I'll work less hours; the list goes on.

The reason that people don't maintain these goals is because they are not truly focused and that's because they consider this goal to be something they *should* do, as opposed to thinking they *must* do it.

Goals suggest to us that something needs to change, but maybe we don't always need to change something, we just need to tweak it to be the best version of ourselves.

When we set an intention, this implies it is something we *must* do, because we intend to take action and when we intend to take action we can really focus our energy on developing our strategy for realizing all our dreams, wants and needs. What do you intend to do?

Let's PERFORM

Exercise #5

Visualize Your Intentions

Visualizing your intentions helps you to not just get focused but to also follow through with actions to reach your goals.

In Exercise #3 you defined your weekly goals. Now take seven minutes to imagine these are your intentions (you *must* do them) and visualize them by doing the following.

- Sit comfortably with feet flat on the floor and your back straight and close your eyes.
- Visualize yourself undertaking each intention. See it in full detail and try to engage all your senses, seeing, hearing, tasting, smelling and feeling what it is like to complete that goal. When you have completed this move on to the next intention on your list.

- Note down how it feels to achieve and live that intention in your visualization.

This exercise not only helps you visualize your intention being completed and consequently increases focus and motivation, it also helps to reduce feelings of stress and improve your performance, plus a boost to your energy levels.

Forgive and Let Go

"My focus is to forget the pain of life. Forget the pain, mock the pain, reduce it and laugh."
Jim Carrey, Actor

Something that gets in the way of us focusing on our intentions and goals and being motivated is our mind being caught up in past memories of when things didn't go to plan. We try and live our new stories from the perspective of an old identity and often, when we think of these past memories we develop new emotions which we attach to the event.

We need to set ourselves free from the pain of the past and not be burdened by the heavy emotions which we attach to our new story, meaning that we can not be fully effective in performing at our best.

In order to be more focused we need to forgive, both others and ourselves. This isn't always easy and takes work, but that work is worth it, because when we forgive and let go we set ourselves free from the pain and release the negative emotions and energy. We open ourselves up to a new realm of possibilities, we can enjoy life, we become more resilient, optimistic about our future, we build better future relationships and we strengthen our mindset to one of growth; yes, we can truly PERFORM.

Pain and suffering doesn't necessary go away, but forgiving allows us to embrace the experience and use it to grow, learn and flourish from. Whether it's a situation, a person, a failure, there is always a lesson to be had and we get to create that lesson and move forwards with it, so it's in our interest to make it a good one.

Let's try releasing that pain and those old stories to allow more space for focus and freedom.

Let's PERFORM
Exercise #6
Write a Letter

Learning to forgive is really important because sometimes we are actually self-sabotaging ourselves by holding on to past events. This is a quick exercise to release some of that pain and hurt to allow more space in our minds to focus.

Set aside seven minutes (or more), set a timer and write the following letter. We are not going to send this letter but we are going to release the negative feelings and energy that is holding you back from truly focusing on your life and goals.

Imagine you are writing a letter to someone who has hurt, upset or wronged you in the past. For seven minutes write about a time when you felt this hurt, writing about how it made you feel in the moment and any feelings you are still feeling about the situation.

Write about what you wish the person had done instead and what you wish you were experiencing now.

End the letter with empathy, love and forgiveness, stating *"I understand, I love you, I forgive you."*

Once written, take the piece of paper you have written the letter on and tear it up and put it in the bin, or through a shredding machine. If safe to do so, even put it on a fire and watch it disappear, taking with it all your negative feelings, energy and hurt.

You have now released this energy from yourself to gain more focus, clarity and motivation. You may not maintain a relationship with this person, but you have now released yourself from the burden of hurt.

How does this feel?

Train your Brain!

"One reason so few of us achieve what we truly want is that we never direct our focus; we never concentrate our power. Most people dabble their way through life, never deciding to master anything in particular."
Tony Robbins, author and speaker

We have the capacity to train our brains. With consistent thoughts and actions our brain can reorganize itself by creating new neural pathways based on our experiences; it's called *neuroplasticity*.

That means our old story, our old strategies, don't have to be our new ones. We literally have the power to change how we think, feel and behave.

We need to condition our thoughts and actions to be highly effective for us and sometimes we just have to fake it until we make it, and in that time our brain starts to believe its new truth.

For example, if you don't have a lot of self-confidence and are scared of public speaking, if you keep working beyond the fear and stand up and talk to people anyway, your brain will re-wire itself and eventually you will realize you're doing it and you're not scared.

The brain is very cool! The power and efficacy of our beliefs and actions is dependent on the stories we tell ourselves.

Did you know you can use your body to influence your mind, which then influences your beliefs and consequently leads to more positive outcomes?

The way we communicate is vital and 65% of our communication is non-verbal (ie. our body language). We focus a lot on how we communicate with others but sometimes we don't focus on how we communicate with ourselves, but that matters because it affects our mood and how we PERFORM.

It's time to address this fact and use our body to tell our mind that we are strong and capable and to feel focused. How are we going to do this? By holding a simple high power pose which allows our body to tell our brain we are full of confidence and focused.

This may seem like woo-woo nonsense but actually there is real science behind this concept. Holding this pose for two minutes has been shown to raise your Testosterone level by 20% (meaning more power and confidence), reduce your Cortisol level by 25% (meaning stress reduction and boosted mood) and increases your risk tolerance by 33% (making you more likely to 'go for it' and perform at your best). A reduction in Cortisol has a real positive impact on our mood, and so does a rise in

Testosterone which not only improves our mood, it can also give us:

- a rise in sex drive
- stronger bones
- less fat and more muscle
- a healthier heart and blood
- better verbal memory and potential
- reduction in proneness to Alzheimer's

This simple, quick and easy change in your physiology which trains our brain for more confidence and focus, actually changes your bio-chemistry too.

So, if you have a performance, exam, job interview, big event or just need that boost in mood or confidence and to focus more, give this exercise a try now.

Let's PERFORM
Exercise #7
The Power Pose

This is a quick two minute exercise to train your brain and feel more focused and confident.

Simply engage in a power pose for 2 minutes. This *wonder woman* pose is the best known but any high power pose is good.

- Stand with your feet hip width apart.

- Put your hands on hips.

- Point your chin to the sky and look up.

- Breathe deeply in and out of your belly.

Hold this pose for two minutes.

How do you feel?

"Always remember your focus determines your reality." George Lucas, American filmmaker

What we think we believe and where we aim our focus is where our energy goes.

In order to perform at our best we need to be focused on what we want. We need to get our mind in a good state, create a motivating story and design an effective strategy.

With these three elements in place; state, story and strategy, our focus will be highly effective and we can really start to PERFORM.

… and remember… where your focus goes, your energy flows.

I hope that gives you some motivation. Now it's time to go and get focused to PERFORM.

OPTIMISM

the way to... Create Optimism!

"There are only two ways to live your life. One is as though nothing is a miracle. The other is as though everything is a miracle."

Albert Einstein, Physicist

Here's two important facts about optimism I want you to remember from the outset.

- Optimism is not just blind hope or wishful thinking; and

- Optimism can be created.

Optimism is an emotion which can be learned and cultivated to give a positive perspective. It is complementary to hope and with an optimistic outlook we are in a better position to enhance wellness and cultivate a positive perspective.

Contrary to the belief of pessimists (those who have a tendency to see the worst in situations or think the worst will happen), optimists expect better outcomes. This doesn't mean that they live in a world of toxic positivity, thinking everything will always be amazing, after all positivity is not the concept that everything will be OK, it's knowing you can be OK regardless of what happens. Pessimism is fear; optimism is courage and in the words of psychologist Dr. Susan David *"Courage is not the absence of fear; courage is fear walking."*

Optimism is intelligent thinking; it builds resilience against stressful events and boosts emotional fitness to protect mental health by boosting positive emotions which self-perpetuate, building more for even more resilience and flourishing. At its essence, optimism means that an attitude and behaviours can be chosen by recognizing negative self-talk and self-criticism and reframing this to bring more self-compassion and kindness. When we are kinder to ourselves it builds self-confidence and having more confidence opens us up to the possibility of optimism and a more hopeful future.

Be Kind to Yourself

"Many of the qualities that come so effortlessly to dogs – loyalty, devotion, selflessness, unflagging optimism, unqualified love – can be elusive to humans." John Grogan, writer

More often we will be kinder to others before we extend that kindness to ourselves. Think about it a moment, how often have you told someone *"it will be OK"* or *"things will get better"* when something doesn't go to plan, yet in the same situation you've told yourself *"what an idiot"* or *"how could you be so stupid?"* We are not always kind to ourselves, in fact sometimes we are outright mean!

We need to extend more self-compassion and kindness to ourselves. For clarity, self-kindness (or self-care) is when we treat ourselves kindly whereas self-compassion is regarding yourself kindly. Simply put one is *doing* and the other *thinking.* Kindness does and compassion thinks.

The reason for more self-compassion and kindness is because it empowers us; it builds self-confidence, resilience and emotional fitness, and the people that are emotionally fitter, more resilient and kinder to themselves are less likely to slip into self-loathing and experience poor mental health and even mental illness.

Self-compassion and kindness protect our mental health. They also help us from burning out.

Burnout doesn't just happen to us. It builds gradually - we ignore the early signs and keep pushing through until our body and mind can't handle it anymore. Burnout is the consequence of continued exposure to stress which result in physical and mental exhaustion.

Now, stress isn't always bad for us; we need some stress and good stress (or eustress) helps us achieve amazing things. We all have different stress capacities, hence why some people may flourish and some languish when exposed to the same situations, but issues generally arise when we don't have the strategies to manage our stress.

Burnout builds in stages and it's important we don't ignore those early signs and prioritise self-care, self-compassion and self-kindness at every opportunity.

The Seven Stages of Burnout are:

- **Stage 1** - Insecurity leading to a strong desire to prove yourself and work harder to achieve this.
- **Stage 2**- Working harder, not smarter, meaning you neglect your own needs.
- **Stage 3** - You don't take accountability, therefore blaming others for situations and you deny problems that arise due to stress.
- **Stage 4** - Your focus shifts, you work more and withdraw from family, friends and social life.
- **Stage 5** - Your personality and behaviour changes meaning you don't feel like yourself which affects relationships with the self and others.
- **Stage 6** - You feel numb and alone which can lead to using unhelpful coping strategies, depression or anxiety.
- **Stage 7** - You have no capacity left and are emotionally and physically exhausted, meaning full burnout.

Let's PERFORM
Exercise #1
Letter of Self-Compassion

In order to have a more optimistic perspective we need to show ourselves more compassion.

Set aside some time to write a letter of self compassion following these steps:

• Choose an aspect of your life or yourself that you dislike or criticize. It may be your career, appearance or relationships. Write down how this makes you feel. What thoughts or stories come up for you when you think of it?

• Now imagine someone who loves you unconditionally, sees your strengths and is always there for you. They are kind, forgiving and embrace and support you as you are. Who is this person for you?

•   Write a short letter to yourself from the perspective of this person. What do they say? How do they show compassion? How do they support you? Once written, set the letter aside.

•   When a little time has passed (at least an hour) come back to the letter and read it. How does this make you feel? Feel the support, compassion and encouragement and let it sink in.

•   Next time you feel negative thoughts, disempowered, lacking self-kindness or a less than optimistic outlook, read the letter and let the positive words flood you with feelings of compassion, love and support. This encouragement is the first step to building self-confidence and feeling more empowered.

Embracing Anxiety

"Choose to be optimistic. It feels better."
Dalai Lama, Spiritual leader

Recognizing negative self-talk and self-criticism is important in this context as self-criticism is related to the perception of a threat which can lead to anxiety.

Whilst anxiety is the brain's natural response to perceived danger, issues such as anxiety disorders occur when this response is out of alignment with the threat in question.

The brain is not always fantastic at differentiating between levels of threat though, which means sometimes we need to manually override our response to anxiety. We don't always have to go with a *fight or flight* response; we could utilize a *challenge* or *tend and befriend* response.

These choices allow us to learn, grow and connect from our experiences rather than just fighting, fleeing, freezing or in extreme cases engaging in a *flop* response when we can literally just faint.

Ever seen a highly stressed goat? Their stress response to anxiety is *flop* mode. They look to have literally fainted. However, they do not lose consciousness but in an attempt to flee when scared they can experience their muscles stiffening up for a short time, meaning they fall over! True story!

But physiologically (meaning relating to the way our bodies feel and work) nerves and excitement have the same response, therefore when optimism is present, it can be a contribution to managing a perceived threat to give a different response of excitement through reframing the thoughts from being nervous to excited.

The ABC model is a renowned exercise in Cognitive Behavioral Therapy (CBT) and is developed on the mindset that external events (A) do not cause emotions (C), but beliefs about events (B) do. Emotions and behaviours (C: Consequences) are not directly determined by life events (A: Activating Events), but rather by the way we think about these events and they are cognitively processed and evaluated (B: Beliefs).

When we experience an event and our behavior is influenced by our beliefs rather than rationality we want to try and dispute these thoughts in order to have a new effect. ie. we are turning the irrational belief into a rational belief, and now we have a healthier consequence of the belief as a result.

By adding the steps of disputation and adding a new effect we turn the ABC model into the ABCDE model and this reframing of our thoughts allows for a more optimistic outlook on life.

Let's look at how we can reframe our thoughts in this exercise, which is handy to use anytime we think we are not responding to an actual event but are, in fact, reacting to our emotions about an event.

Let's PERFORM
Exercise #2
ABCDE Reframe

Take seven minutes to consider this activity.

A – Activating Event – What is the Activating Event? What happened? What did you or others do? How did you feel about it?

C – Consequence – What are you feeling right now? List the emotions and feelings you are experiencing. Are you behaving in a way that is unhelpful to you (out of frustration, fear or anger?).

B – Belief – What beliefs do you have about the activating event? Which of these beliefs are helpful to you? Which beliefs are unhelpful?

D – Disputation – Dispute the unhelpful beliefs. What evidence do you have for these beliefs?

E – New Effect – How can you replace these beliefs? What helpful strategy can you implement? How do you feel about the Activating Event with these new beliefs?

See it Clearly

"Optimism means better than reality;
pessimism means worse than reality.
I'm a realist."
Margaret Atwood, writer

We need to get a vision in order to learn, grow and contribute and let's face it, learning, growing and contributing are three things that are going to help us become emotionally fitter and flourish.

Our vision needs to be of what we want, then we can develop our pathway to achieving our goals and also become aware of the potential issues along the way.

When we are looking at those potential issues or holdups we need to see them as accurately as possible, seeing them for what they are and not worse than they are.

Optimism is intelligent thinking; it's seeing situations with possibility and hope whilst also understanding the potential for difficulty and by balancing those elements, we put into play the actions to help us overcome challenges.

When we consider our visions, our hopes, dreams and goals, we want to create the best possible version of our future and ourselves.

By focusing on our best possible self we have the power to increase our wellness and see the world not just realistically but optimistically. This also means we boost our mood positively too and all the positive emotions we feel... they empower us with confidence and kindness.

But how often do you visualize the best possible version of yourself? Indeed, have you ever visualized it consistently? I don't mean just see it but really feel it, engaging all your senses and emerging yourself in the sensory emotions of what that truly feels like?

Maybe you've tried a few times, or maybe it's never occurred to you to do, but there is such value in consistently seeing that vision clearly and realistically.

Let's give it a try.

Let's PERFORM

Exercise #3

Your Best Possible Self

Set aside seven minutes to try this activity.

•   Imagine in 12 months' time you are the best possible version of yourself. Think about your values, what's important to you and the positive changes you would like to make.

•   Visualize this version of you in full color detail. What does it look like? Feel like? Sound like? Taste like? Smell like? Who is in your life? Where are you? What are you doing?

•   Bring this image to full life in your mind and enjoy the experience before coming back into the present moment.

•   Write down the details of what you visualized. This can help you gain clarity on your goals and intentions and the steps you need to take to achieve them.

How do you feel?

Looking Back

"Hope is definitely not the same thing as optimism. It is not the conviction that something will turn out well, but the certainty that something makes sense, regardless of how it turns out."
Václav Havel, former President of Czechoslovakia

Optimism, growth and freedom are all dependent on looking forwards, and whilst creating a forward motion is important for a flourishing life, we should never be scared to look backwards.

Our experiences shape us; some we want to hold onto as they made us happy, others we want to let go of as they fail to bring us joy or inflict hurt and pain.

But there is a lesson in everything and looking at our past experiences, especially the positive ones, and reflecting on them can help us not only grow but to develop a sense of determination, possibility, courage and resilience.

Reflection can help us perform at our best as we take the lessons, embrace them and move forwards with them to create optimism for the future.

Let's PERFORM
Exercise #4
Positive Reminiscing

This is a simple activity you can try for seven minutes.

• Think about a moment from your past that brings up positive emotions in you.

• Visualize this version of you in full color detail. What does it look like? Feel like? Sound like? Taste like? Smell like? Who is in your life? Where are you? What are you doing?

• Focus on the pleasant and happy feelings. Hold this focus for a few minutes.

• Write down the emotions and feelings that you felt when the event happened and how you feel about the event now, reflecting on it.

How do you feel? This boost in positive emotions allows us to feel more optimistic moving forwards.

Get Practicing!

"While we may not be able to control all that happens to us, we can control what happens inside us."
Benjamin Franklin, Founding Father of the USA

As already stated, optimism can be created. It is a learned behavior and one worth learning because it has so many benefits for living a flourish life and protecting our mental health.

The last two exercises have seen us visualize our best possible self and reminisce on positive past events, but to perform at our best and bring our optimism to life, we need to mentally rehearse our strategy for turning our thoughts into reality.

Mental rehearsal is often used by athletes and musicians, but is a great tool for anyone; helping us be more optimistic and confident with a variety of life events from job interviews to presentations, live performances to teaching.

This technique can help us develop our skills and mindset and is a highly valuable asset in our armory of tools for peak performance; hence why it's so popular and effective in the world of sport.

One study around mental rehearsal presented research conducted by the University of Chicago with basketball players. The intention was to see if mental rehearsal could help players improve their free throws by just visualizing themselves taking and scoring free throws, with no actual basketball played, over the course of 30 days the players saw a 23% improvement in their free throw rate... without touching a single basketball!

As a musician I was once advised by a well-respected and successful professional that 95% of your practice is done without the instrument.

Not only does mental rehearsal improve your mindset and skill, it also boosts your confidence and consequently your proneness for optimism and achieving a state of *Flow*. It can make that presentation, interview or performance be the absolute best it can be.

Let's PERFORM

Exercise #5

Mental Rehearsal

For seven minutes try this activity.

• Consider a forthcoming performance, match, race, interview, presentation or event where you want to perform at your best.

• Take a deep breath in and out.

• First visualize an event in full detail when you performed at your best; when you were confident and everything went to plan. Enjoy those positive feelings.

• Now think of your forthcoming event. Consider it in full detail where you are at your best and everything goes to plan. Run through the whole process from your arrival to your departure.

- If you would like move your body as you will in the real event. Imagine it all in real time and focus on being your best.

- What emotions do you feel? Does it feel good?

- Write down anything you notice.

By first anchoring ourselves in a positive state by reflecting on a successful and positive past event we raise our energy, focus and optimism levels to allow our mental rehearsal to be highly effective.

In the build up to your chosen event, re-visit this exercise, mentally rehearsing every day until it becomes completely familiar and you have shifted your energy from feeling anxious to excited. Now you are ready to perform at your best and you haven't just practiced until you can do it, you've practiced until it can't go wrong.

You're Done

"My optimism wears heavy boots and is loud."
Henry Rollins, singer

Sometimes it feels hard to be optimistic about the future because we are so wrapped up in the present and overwhelmed by what we have to do. Many people opt to deal with plethora of things they have to do by creating *To Do* lists and these can be really helpful in keeping us organized and keeping overwhelm at bay.

But does the well-used *To Do* list actually hinder our capacity for optimism? Is it possible that once we have listed the numerous tasks we need to do that actually that seemingly never-ending list can make us feel even more overwhelmed?

There is no doubting that a list helps us gain clarity, be organized and often feel very satisfied when we cross things off. But what if there was something even better to help fuel optimism?

I give you the *Done* list*!*

Let's PERFORM
Exercise #6
The Done List

This is a twist on the traditional *To Do* list that gives extra feelings of possibility, positivity and optimism! It's even more satisfying than crossing off items on your *To Do* list, is super simple and it only takes a few minutes. Ready?

•   On a piece of paper write the title *Done* at the top.

•   Every time you complete a job, task or item on your *To Do* list, write it on your *Done* list and have a little mini celebration or high-5 with yourself! Yes, celebrate that task no matter how small or big!

•   Keep adding to the *Done* list and watch it grow!

When we see what we have achieved we grow feelings of confidence and pride and when we celebrate ourselves we multiply those *feel good* feelings all the more without the overwhelm of everything else there is to do. If you're ever feeling overwhelmed by your *To Do* list, simply take a look at your *Done* list and celebrate your brilliance.

It's Non-Negotiable

"You have to look at the future with optimism instead of negative ideas. Take the good and the bad and face it head on." Goldie Hawn, Actor

Difficult things will happen in our lives, that is a fact. At some point we will all experience something distressing but that should never move us from thinking intelligently and intelligent thinking means using optimism as an asset for a flourishing life.

Optimism should be a non-negotiable; it's going to help you perform at your best and yes, peak performance takes work, but anything worth having takes work, be that careers, goals or relationships.

This book has talked a lot about visualizing our best possible self, our best performance and reminiscing positively and now it's time to make those best possible future events non-negotiable. Sign up to the idea that they are possible and don't let your commitment falter. You will thank yourself.

Let's PERFORM
Exercise #7
A Non-Negotiable Day

This is a fun little activity that you need to make a *must* in the next few weeks.

To get you into the habit of living optimistically and making the best version of yourself and future events non-negotiable, you are going to get in some practice by scheduling a non-negotiable day.

• Make a list of all the things you would like to do for you; they may be fun, exciting, something you've been meaning to do for ages or adventurous. Remember this is purely for you.

• Choose one thing from your list you can do in the next few weeks.

- Visualize it in your mind in full detail. How does it make you feel actually doing it?

- Schedule it in your diary for a day in the next month.

This is **non-negotiable** so commit to it and enjoy!

"Positive thinking is the notion that if you think good thoughts, things will work out well. Optimism is the feeling of thinking things will be well and be hopeful."
Martin Seligman, founder of positive psychology

There we have it, a short guide on the way to not just be optimistic but to actually create optimism. This is within your power to actively develop the skills and behaviours and be an active participant in a more optimistic life, full of possibility, enjoyment and happiness.

Optimism is intelligent thinking and you are an intelligent thinker. When your energy feels low, just remember that fact and go and create some more optimism... it is a renewable source of energy.

RELATIONSHIPS

the way to... Build Relationships

"Falling in love and having a relationship are two different things." Keanu Reeves, Actor

When we talk about relationships we are not just talking about love or intimate relationships. We are also talking about friendships, colleague relationships, relationships with family, how we connect to strangers, mentor relationships and of course, the relationship we prioritise least; the one with ourself.

Relationships can be referred to as feelings of love, kindness and support from others; connections that contribute to higher levels of wellness, emotional fitness and can be a protective factor for mental and physical health.

Whilst having good connection with others is important, we cannot forget the importance of having a good relationship with ourself too in order to boost self-confidence and self-trust and this increase in confidence through self-compassion and self-kindness means less chance self-criticism and self-loathing and consequently, this connection with ourself equally protects our mental and physical health.

Through the course of my life I have had a wide spectrum of relationships that have been good and bad. I have experienced the happiest, most loving and supportive relationships as well as the most volatile, destructive and abusive ones.

I have tried hard at maintaining relationships and I have also let some go both intentionally and not intentionally. At times I have given too much and sometimes I've not given enough. I've excelled and failed... and these relationships, they're not just reflective of connections with other people... my relationship with myself has been through all these phases too.

Let's PERFORM
Exercise #1
Valuing Myself

Too often we focus on our negatives and less on our good aspects. In order to build healthy relationships with ourself and others we need to value ourselves.

Take seven minutes to consider these questions and write down your thoughts.

- What qualities do I love in myself?
- What qualities do I notice in myself that I would find attractive in other people?
- What are my favorite memories of time when I have been alone in my own company?
- When have I shown myself real care and compassion?
- Based on the above, why do I value myself?

Reflect on the answers to your questions and if ever your self-esteem feels low, remind yourself of these amazing values that you have and admire.

It Starts with Me...

"If you have the ability to love, love yourself first." Charles Bukowski, Poet

"You look great."
"I just found this outfit in the back of my closet."

"What you did was amazing."
"I didn't do anything special that others wouldn't do."

"You are so wise."
"It's nothing you wouldn't hear from someone else."

"You are so successful."
"Not really, I'm just getting by."

"I wish I was you."

"You really don't."

Self-deprecation – described in the dictionary as *modesty about or criticism of oneself.* It's what we can do when we feel uncomfortable receiving compliments and kindness from others.

It feels hard to say *thank you* or receive the kind words. Why? Because we don't value ourself, and that's why we started this book by identifying those values.

When given compliments often we either self-deprecate or deflect with humor rather than accepting the words with grace and gratitude. This isn't because we are bad people; it's because we've often been raised to dim our lights, be small or live in scarcity.

We shouldn't brag, boast or celebrate what we do have and instead we should bond over lack and weakness. But all this does is make us love ourselves less and lowers our levels of confidence and self-esteem.

We would likely always extend compliments and kindness to others, yet we fall foul of extending the same to ourself, opting for strategies that keep us in that small, dark place. But when we value ourselves, that is when we can truly accept love and kindness from others because it feels natural as we are so used to extending it to ourselves.

Let's PERFORM
Exercise #2
The Mirror

When we learn to accept kindness and compliments from ourselves, we can accept them from others more uncomfortably or at least with grace and gratitude and a simple response of *thank you.*

We need to get comfortable with the uncomfortable notion of self-kindness to help build self-esteem and confidence and there is no simpler way than being kind to yourself.

In a morning when you get ready for your day, spend a few minutes undertaking this mirror exercise.

It will likely feel very uncomfortable at first but that's OK. When we stick with it we will move through that discomfort and emerge with more self-love, self-esteem and self-confidence. It will strengthen the relationship with ourself.

Choose a mirror in your house and try the following:

- Look into the mirror so your whole face is visible. If possible find a full length mirror so you can see your whole body.

- Take a few deep breaths in and out through your nose to ground and center yourself.

- Say to yourself *I love you* and say it with meaning. Repeat over and over again for a few minutes, looking straight into your own eyes. Be aware of the tone and timbre of your voice so your words and voice are congruent – in other words they match and you sound as if you truly mean what you are saying. Say *I love you* to yourself in the same way you would say it to someone you passionately loved and cared for.

How does it feel?

It may feel silly or uncomfortable at first but persist until it feels good. You can extend the exercise by extending other compliments to yourself, such as *you look healthy* or *you are strong.* Think of compliments you would say to others and extend them to yourself on repeat until you feel your self-esteem increase.

People Pleasing

"When you say 'yes' to others make sure you aren't saying 'no' to yourself." Paulo Coelho, Writer

I am an inherent people pleaser... hang on, let me rephrase that... I *was* an inherent people pleaser.

Over-giving and consistently putting others' needs ahead of my own was a serious cause of low moods, depression and social anxiety for me. I felt that in order to have my basic needs of love, care and support met that I had to do everything in my power to make life easier and better for others.

I WAS WRONG!

People pleasing is a fast-route to poor mental health. Yes, of course we want to be considerate of the needs of others, we want to help and support where we can, we want to be generous where possible, but it can never be at the detriment of your own health and needs.

Ask yourself honestly where you are over-giving. Does every kind and generous action feel good to you? Are you over-giving to your closest friends, your boss, your work, your partner, your children or your family? Just because they are so close or important to you does not make it any more acceptable.

Our need to please is really a need to *belong* and that need to belong has been hard-wired into us over thousands of years. We have been raised to be courteous and put other people's needs ahead of our own, but when we take this too far, when we overdo this politeness or care taking, that is when we can slip into the realms of people pleasing. Our *need* to please becomes greater than the actual desire to help and support out of good intent. Our fear then keeps us from saving ourself. Our fears are of being judged, becoming disconnected or not being needed and our internal voice gets louder telling us untruths such as *they will be angry, they will hate me, they don't like me, I am a terrible person...* and oh so quickly we spiral into guilt and shame.

So the only option is to people please... to give more than we get and to keep giving to feel needed?
WRONG... it's not the only option. There is another option where we build healthier relationships with ourself and others by making sure we are meeting our own needs and calling our people pleasing behaviours into question and replace with kindness and generosity and not over-giving.

It's time to reflect on your needs and behaviours and to call any people pleasing tendencies into question.

When we can recognize these thoughts and behaviours we can check in with ourselves that we are not over-giving and potentially risking our health, relationships and satisfaction by giving too much to others unnecessarily.

Let's PERFORM

Exercise #3

Meet my Needs

Set aside seven minutes to reflect on the following questions. Note down your thoughts on paper.

- What experiences led you to needing to people please? Was it a fear of criticism, judgement or rejection?

- What needs do you have that often go unmet?

- Why do you undervalue your own needs?

- Do you over-compensate for your own needs by over-giving to others, be that in time, energy, money or material things?

- How would it feel to not over-give but to gift these things to others?

- How would it feel to gift these things to yourself?

What did you notice?

Boundaries

"Compassionate people ask for what they need. They say no when they need to, and when they say yes, they mean it. They're compassionate because their boundaries keep them out of resentment."
Brené Brown, Researcher, author and speaker

Boundaries are the limits we set for ourselves in our relationships and it's an essential thing to do for healthier relationships.

There is always the option to say *NO* in our relationships. We don't always have to say *yes* to everything and saying *no* can be the healthiest choice, even if it feels counterintuitive, selfish or uncomfortable.

The ability to say *no* comes from having our boundaries firmly set in place.

Having boundaries that we implement and stick to is so important for forging great relationships and for protecting our mental health care.

As adults we often put boundaries in place for children to adhere to, we even put them in place for our pets, but we seem less open to implementing them into our own lives.

Our boundaries show people what is and what is not acceptable to us. It shows them we have respect for our own values and needs and we will only tolerate relationships and actions that support and honor these needs and values.

Boundaries can be big or small; the important thing is that they're consistent. Once implemented we need to maintain them and hold strong, not letting anyone disrespect them, because once they are broken down, it is easier for us to disrespect them too.

Whether it's adhering to strict working hours, putting your contactable hours on an email signature, asking people to only contact you by text message and not a phone call or letting go of people who don't meet your exact needs, boundaries come in a multitude of shapes and sizes but they all have two important roles; to keep you safe and to meet your needs.

Let's PERFORM

Exercise #4

Draw your Boundary

Take seven minutes to visualize your boundaries. Take a piece of paper and follow these steps:

Step 1 - Reflect on life as it is now and answer the following.

- What is making you feel stressed?
- What do you look forward to each day?
- What fills you with dread?
- What or who fuels your energy?
- What or who drains you?
- What or who makes you feel safe?

Step 2 – draw a large circle on your piece of paper. Inside the circle write everything that makes you feel safe and less stressed.

This may be being active, reading, stroking a pet, a partner who protects you, having a routine, conversations with friends, nutritious eating, having time for you, hugs and intimacy.

Step 3 – outside the circle write everything that makes you feel unsafe, stressed, uncomfortable or unsafe.

This could be worrying about things, a lack of trust from a partner, violation of personal space or privacy such as someone reading your messages. It could be fear of judgement, criticism on your parenting, working or living choices, overworking, messiness in your living space, people contacting you about work at the weekend or people asking to borrow money.

Your boundaries are now drawn. Use these to set those limits of acceptability between you and other people.

How does it feel to set your boundaries?

Get Connected

"Invisible threads are the strongest ties."
Friedrich Nietzsche, German philosopher

Positive relationships with the self are vital, but so to are our relationships with others. One of the most important factors in human flourishing is building close relationships with others and contrary to some beliefs, being strict with our boundaries does not keep people out of our lives, it welcomes the right people in.

Identifying and implementing our boundaries can often make others feel uncomfortable, but if our boundaries are in line with our values then the comfort of others is not our concern. Our priority should be ourself and when we take care of ourself first, we can be better and stronger for others and the right people who will understand, support, care and love us will show themselves.

Life is not about having all the people, it's about having the right people.

Think about the oxygen mask analogy; put your own oxygen mask on first before helping someone else with theirs. We can't effectively help someone else survive if we can't breathe.

Never forget you are worthy of prioritising yourself. You are strong and you should allow yourself to shine bright and when you give yourself this permission you strengthen your relationship with yourself enough to foster better connections with others.

A sense of connection is key to healthy living and when we have fostered self-confidence and empowerment through self-compassion and kindness we can help others.

This is a self-perpetuating cycle too. The more we help ourselves, the more capacity we have to help others which in turn brings more help and support back to us.

We build a network that helps us flourish and thrive. I like to adopt a policy of helping others get what they desire because this helps me to receive what I desire and strive for too. But this is only possible because I extend myself enough self-compassion to know my values and implement my boundaries.

What time and experience has taught me is I am much richer for connecting with the right people who raise my energy, raise my ambitions and who challenge me to be the best version of myself and for that I am grateful.

Consider who makes you feel good, who adds value to your life and who is really there for you when you need it most. These may not be people you have known for years, but it may be new people in your life who stepped up when you needed it most or you were there for them.

Open yourself up to new relationships, new possibilities and new connections on a deeper level, based on your values and with your boundaries respected.

Let's PERFORM
Exercise #5
Random Act of Kindness

A great way to connect with others and build relationships is through kindness. Not in a contrived way because we feel we have to, but in an exciting, generous (but not over-giving) type of way.

This activity need only take a couple of minutes and it will fuel you with positive feelings whilst connecting deeply with others.

Today, I want you to undertake a random act of kindness. That may be buying a drink for the stranger behind you in a coffee shop queue, it might be taking a meal round to a friend's house, it might be sending a funny postcard. Or you might think bigger and take someone on an unexpected trip!

Don't over-give; this can be a small gesture so work within your boundaries, means and with your values. The important thing is that it is random and unexpected to someone.

Rich and Wealthy

"Wealth is the ability to fully experience life."
Henry David Thoreau, Poet and philosopher

Deeper, more connected relationships with yourself and others make you richer and whilst that feeling of wealth is not always about money, our relationships with money have a huge impact on how we feel.

Wealth is a complex mix of elements (including money) that allow us to experience life to the full, but our relationship with money can be unhealthy and consequently hinders our ability to live a fulfilled life.

There is no shame in wanting, loving or receiving money, yet many people live in a mindset of scarcity which gets in the way of them experiencing an abundant and fulfilled life.

We are taught not to highlight our riches for fear of bragging, flaunting or showing-off in front of those who are less well-off.

When we become small and default to a scarcity mindset to appease others, all we are doing is sabotaging our own possibilities and opportunities to live rich, fulfilled and wealthy lives. We should be able to live our biggest, richest and most fulfilled lives without shame and rather than hiding our fortune and wealth (be that financial, material, physical, emotional or spiritual) we should share our wins in order to inspire and motivate others; show them that with an attitude of abundance and gratitude combined with taking the right action, money is available to everyone. It is a renewable resource.

This is often a difficult concept to understand when we are living from hand to mouth, in poverty and surrounded by stories of recessions and cost of living difficulties, but when we choose to exit our scarcity mindset and trade it for one of abundance, when we do the work, our relationship with money can become a lot healthier and more positive and the possibility of a wealthy life moves closer into focus.

Let's PERFORM
Exercise #6
Abundant Affirmations

Affirmations are short positive statements that help us re-wire our minds. Used consistently they are highly effective for building positive emotions and building relationships.

Set a timer for seven minutes for the following activity. Sit comfortably with your eyes closed, feet on the floor and your hands resting on your lap, palms facing upwards. Repeat the following positive statements:

- I am abundant

- I am worthy of receiving money

- I love money and money loves me

- Money flows easily to me

- It is safe to love money

- I am worthy of being happy and prosperous

- I am open to receiving

Repeat this exercise daily and notice how your relationship with money strengthens positively.

Let it Go!

"If you're brave enough to say goodbye, life will reward you with a new hello." Paulo Coelho, Writer

Not every relationship we have is meant to be forever. How can it be? As we learn and grow our needs change, we change and our goals change and not everyone or everything we have a relationship with will learn and grow at the same speed. These changes mean that at some stage our values, beliefs, psychological and physical needs develop. Trying to make old relationships fit this new version of ourself is not always possible or even necessary and staying stuck can keep us small and less likely to live a truly fulfilled life performing at our best.

It is common for people to try and hold on to relationships because of a sense of duty, but this can lead to resentment and hurtful behaviours. Being open to change means maintaining healthy relationships in the best way possible and for the duration they were meant for.

This also means letting go of relationship patterns with yourself that don't empower you, like overriding your inner critic and changing your habits to be healthier ones.

Some people will stay with you forever, but some are only meant to guide you through certain chapters. Even in the throes of grief and loss it is possible to recognize that the person we lost was with us to guide us when we needed it most and they leave us to travel on independently both stronger and more empowered as a consequence of having them in our life. It doesn't make their departure any less painful, but it does allow us to create meaning from their death.

Sometimes we have no option but to lose relationships, be that through death, a lack of care or the decisions of others, but sometimes we have to be courageous enough to let go of disempowering relationships; those that don't serve the current version of ourself.

If a relationship is consistently lacking the elements that meet our basic psychological needs of autonomy (the need to feel ownership of our behaviours), competency (the need to experience mastery, or to perform at our best) and relatedness (the need to feel connected to others) or it fails to bring us safety (be that physical, emotional or financial) despite our efforts to address the issues, sometimes the hardest but best thing we can do for our learning and growing self is to let it go.

If a relationship disempowers you in any way you need prioritise yourself and your current needs. You are worthy of living your best life and being the best version of yourself; don't let anyone treat you otherwise... take the action to empower yourself and the right people will join you for the ride.

Let's PERFORM

Exercise #7

Give Yourself a Break

It can be hard to maintain healthy relationships with ourselves and others and sometimes we just need to give ourselves a break.

Take seven minutes to practice this self-compassion break and move away from self-criticism and closer to flourishing.

Sit comfortably with your feet on the floor, close your eyes and think of the situation causing you distress or anxious feelings and say to yourself:

- This is emotional distress. This is what it feels like to me. I can feel the physical and emotional sensations in my breathing, heart rate, hands and mind.

Allow yourself to feel all the sensations then say to yourself:

- Emotional distress is a part of life. Anxiety is a natural response. It is keeping me safe from danger. Everyone feels this way sometimes. It is natural.

Put your hands over your heart, feel the gentle touch of your hands on your chest. Say to yourself:

- I am safe now. Thank you for keeping me safe. I can manage this situation. It is safe for me to have healthy relationships. May I give myself the compassion that I need to perform with ease.

This exercise is not exclusive to relationships and can be adapted for any situation that may be making you feel anxious or emotionally distressed.

"Never above you. Never below you. Always beside you." Walter Winchell, American newspaper columnist

Relationships, be that with yourself, other people, money or behaviours take work. Sometimes they can be uncomfortable and sometimes they test our core strengths, values and beliefs. But with thought, work, compassion and kindness they can be amazing and function at a level that empowers us and support us in the way that we need to be supported.

Stay connected... to yourself, to others and to your intentions. When you stay connected, when you listen to your needs and fulfill the needs of yourself and those in your life, your relationships can flourish, you can live in an abundance of health, happiness and wealth.

That possibility is open to all of us who are prepared to do the work and take the action. Are you ready?

MINDSET

the way to... Choose Your Mindset

"If you can build a muscle, you can

build a mindset."

Jay Shetty, Writer, podcaster and former monk

Growth, fixed, fear, scarcity, 'yes', positive, social, lazy, dream, follower, gratitude, creative, defeatist, confident, money, abundance – these are just some examples of types of mindset and the best thing about a mindset? You get to choose which one you utilize.

A mindset is a person's way of thinking and the mindset we choose dictates the way we approach life, our relationships, success, satisfaction and overall health and happiness.

Our way of thinking doesn't and shouldn't stay the same; it should change and develop as we learn and grow. We have the choice to build and train our mindset in the same way we build and work our muscles... one exercise at a time.

Our mindset impacts our mood, our thoughts, how we speak to ourself and others and our actions.

So what if we chose to make our mindset the best it could possibly be?

What if we chose an attitude of growth, freedom, love and creativity?

What if what was standing between us and reaching our goals was down to the way we think about them?

What if we could determine our outcomes purely by the way we think.

The truth is we can. We have the power to determine our levels of satisfaction and success through the way we think; by simply choosing our mindset.

Let's PERFORM
Exercise #1
Mindset Quiz

This quick quiz can be done in under seven minutes and will help you notice if you have a growth or fixed mindset.

Answer the first five questions and score on the following scale:

0 – strongly agree

1 – agree

2 – disagree

3 – strongly disagree

1. Your intelligence level is something you can't really change?

2. Your personality is a certain way and you can't do much to change it?

3. You have to be born with the ability to be excellent at sports or music?

4. Intelligent people don't need to try hard in life?

5. People commenting on your work and life makes you angry or frustrated?

Answer the next five questions and score on the following scale:

3 – strongly agree
2 – agree
1 – disagree
0 – strongly disagree

6. No matter how much intelligence you have, you can always change it?

7. It is important to constantly learn new things?

8. You appreciate receiving feedback on your life and work?

9. The harder you work the better you get?

10. You can become an expert on anything?

_____Total Score

How to read your score.

22-30: Strong Growth Mindset

17-21: Some growth and fixed beliefs

11-16: Fixed with some growth beliefs

0-10: Strong Fixed Mindset

Believe!

"Whatever the mind can conceive and believe, the mind can achieve." Napoleon Hill, Author

Changing your mindset means challenging your own beliefs and perspectives, or how you look at the world. Our mindset is also based on the beliefs we have about ourselves. In order to fulfil our intentions and reach our goals we need to believe that we can achieve and perform, regardless of what anyone else tells us.

Be unapologetic for the belief you have in yourself and use this feeling to empower your level of self-worth. You are worthy of love and success and even when we are faced with rejection, we need to use the belief in our worth to move forwards with strength.

On a personal level it is our beliefs that stand in the way of us doing the things we *must* do and makes them something we believe we *should* do.

When something is a *should* rather than a *must* we are less likely to fully commit, putting our own fears and self-sabotaging behaviours ahead of what we truly know is best for us.

So why do we self-sabotage? Well self-sabotaging as we like to refer to it is a strategy we develop. Now it's not the most effective or productive strategy, but it is a strategy nonetheless!

Everyone has a deep belief about their own values and when we exceed our own expectations, we become fearful and self-sabotage to put us back in our comfort zone – where we think we belong.

At the other end of the spectrum, when we don't meet our own levels of expectation and values we are faced with two options; we either try and improve (we foster a growth mindset) or we give up and disempower ourselves by believing the story we are useless or not worthy.

The next actions we take (or don't take) are purely based on our perceptions and belief about ourself;
our mindset.

Let's PERFORM
Exercise #2
Scale of Emotions

Take seven minutes to consider this activity and define your scale of emotions.

- Think about a time when you performed at your worst. How did that feel? What emotion can you attach to this experience?
- Now think about a time when you performed at your best. How did that feel? What emotion can you attach to this experience?
- Write them down as below.

[worst emotion]_____[best emotion]

This is your scale of emotions. This is your perception and beliefs; your expectations of what is available to you based on your own experience.

Is it possible that there is something more beyond your *best emotion* at the top of the scale? What one action could you take today to make that possible?

Fear and Scarcity

"Remembering what you've been through and how that has strengthened your mindset can lift you out of a negative brain loop and help you bypass those weak, one-second impulses to give in. Even if you're feeling low and beat down by life right now, I guarantee you can think of a time or two when you overcame odds and tasted success."
David Goggins, former Navy SEAL

The mindsets of fear and scarcity are two of the main culprits for self-sabotaging behaviours. They impact our belief system, what we know to be certain, by fueling us with feelings of worthlessness, hopelessness and helplessness.

If un-managed, it is these feelings that can impact our mental health negatively, seeing it spiral into realms of poor mental health and even mental illness, such as depression and anxiety.

We need to protect our mental health by employing better strategies and that means choosing a more effective mindset.

When we live in a place of fear and scarcity we do not believe we are worthy of good things happening. We do not think we are enough or worthy of more, but this just simply isn't true. We are all worthy of more and there is more available to us, whether that is more love, more connection, more work, more money. It is safe and OK to want more. You are enough, you are worthy. This is not being greedy, it is shifting your mindset from a place of fear and scarcity to one of abundance, fulfilment and growth.

We are not talking about mindless wishing and hoping that things will be better, we are asserting our choice to a mindset that empowers us and helps us develop a strategy to bring more into our lives through consistent action.

Heard of the *Law of Attraction*? This is a real thing. The success of it does not rely on us wishing and hoping but adjusting our mindset to one of abundance and doing the work to bring our thoughts into reality, whilst raising our energy levels to align with the thoughts we have and actions we take. It moves us from a mindset of fear and scarcity to one of abundance.

Let's PERFORM
Exercise #3
The Miracle

This exercise allows us to have seven minutes of thinking big. Set a timer for seven minutes and follow these steps.

Think about the following question:

If there was nothing standing in your way, no fears or limits, what would you do, achieve or receive that you do not have now? Think BIG.

- Write down your thoughts.
- Visualize this big thinking dream.
- How does it feel to receive this dream? Attach an emotion to your thoughts and feelings.

- What one small step could you take today to take you one step closer to this dream and bring it into the reality of your life?

Risk v Reward

"You try something, it doesn't work, and maybe people even criticize you. In a fixed mindset, you say "I tried it, it's over." In a growth mindset , you look for what you've learned." Carol Dweck, Psychologist

Moving from fear and scarcity to abundance means noticing the possibilities that lie ahead for us and not just the limits. Fear limits possibilities.

Our big thinking dream may feel too far away to believe it can become real but with consistent action and a mindset of growth we can steadily move forwards, living in abundance, hope and strength.

Moving towards this new reality with a mindset of growth, positivity and abundance can feel uncomfortable, frightening, scary and again also as if we are not worthy, but that's just your internal voice and mind trying to keep you safe and small. This is normal to feel this way but we have to move beyond that feeling of fear.

In order to be rewarded with our biggest dreams we have to take small risks (and we are not talking about risk taking behaviours that are dangerous or illegal, just small steps beyond our usual limits of belief). There is no reward without risk. But risk doesn't have to be dangerous. Risk can be exciting, something that moves us slightly out of our comfort zone, stretches and strengthens us to be better versions of ourselves.

But be aware of the fact that the further we move towards our goals it will feel like we are increasing our level of risk and that more is at stake. This awareness can lead us to stop or revert in fear again, but choosing our mindset of growth will help us continually move forwards.

Remember our mind will always do more to avoid pain than it will to experience pleasure, so sometimes we need to manually override it in order to reach our goals.

Does it feel risky to reach your goals? Identify that risk, name it and ask yourself if it is a real risk or is your mind just trying to avoid pain. What is more important to you – reaping the reward or avoiding the risk? What mindset can you choose to move closer to being rewarded?

Let's PERFORM
Exercise #4
One Step Closer

Sit down for seven minutes and consider the following.

On a scale of 1 to 10, with 1 being full of fear and having nothing and 10 is your big thinking dream you visualized in Exercise #3, where are you currently?

What would it take to move one step closer to 10 (or stay at 10 if you are already there)?

Write down the action you are going to take and schedule it in your diary. Know it is possible to achieve.

How do you feel about moving closer to achieving your intention, dream or goal?

What If...

"There is freedom waiting for you, on the breezes of the sky, and you ask "What if I fall?" Oh but my darling, what if you fly?"
Erin Hanson, Poet

When we strive for more there is often an internal voice that tries to keep us stuck... the voice that says *but what if I fail? What if it goes wrong? What if I'm judged? What if I'm rejected? What if I'm unloved?*

Those fears of rejection, failure and judgement are natural responses to what our brain perceives as danger. Danger, to our brain, doesn't have to mean a high level of threat, it can be something that is unfamiliar; something we haven't experienced before meaning our brain doesn't have the data on how to respond in that situation.

When these doubts come to mind is when we have to, once again, manually override our mind. We do this by choosing our mindset, by reassuring our brain that whilst something might be an unknown, this doesn't automatically mean it is unsafe.

Yes, this may seem scary but when we have done an internal risk assessment and established that what we are aiming for is not unsafe (though it may have some element of risk required to reap the reward) we can choose the mindset that will best help us reach our goals. Let's put this into context.

Imagine my big thinking dream is to speak on a stage in front of thousands of people, sharing my story and helping people to perform more effectively.

What stops me from achieving this dream goal? Fear of being judged (people may think I'm not qualified enough, that I'm too fat, have an annoying voice etc.), fear of failure (that my ideas don't inspire or help people and I get no future work), fear of rejection and lack of love (people don't resonate with my story and don't like me), fear of it going wrong (I forget my words and people laugh at me).

These fears overwhelm me and my feelings of anxiety tell my brain that this activity is dangerous. It deploys an army of Cortisol, our stress hormone, which floods my body and the outcome is I decide not to take the risk of trying to achieve my dream. It's not possible for me. I'll be better off and safer not trying. I'm not worthy of such attention or success.

Whilst my mood feels low and I experience feelings of worthlessness and hopelessness, my brain is happy it has kept me safe from danger. It did its job.

My mindset of fear, scarcity and defeat was implemented and the strategy associated with that mindset worked. I chose not to even try, thinking there was no point.

But let's run a quick internal risk assessment. Whilst standing on stage in front of thousands of people runs the risk of me being judged (everyone will always have an opinion, we don't need to agree with them or let them be our concern), it runs the risk of failure (I might not inspire everyone, but I could inspire someone), it runs the risk of rejection (not everyone will like me but my story will resonate and connect me with someone) and it runs the risk of going wrong (I could forget my words - but I can have prompts, I could trip – but I will get up and laugh it off, the microphone could stop working – we will replace it) is this dream actually dangerous? No, it isn't.

So what's stopping me doing it? How I think about it... Thinking *what if...* and believing the story my brain tells me. Well, newsflash... your brain is a liar and a little bit dumb – sometimes we need to override it with what we rationally know to be true and we do that by choosing a mindset of possibility, a mindset of growth which allows us to learn and change and a mindset of love that helps us to love ourselves a little more and know we are worthy of achieving our goals.

Let's PERFORM
Exercise #5
Choose Your 'Tude

We are going to choose an attitude of gratitude. This is one of the most simple yet effective tools in our armory of wellness and emotional fitness tools and takes just a few moments.

Each night before you go to bed, write down three things in your day that you are grateful for.

1.

2.

3.

Whilst you can do this at any time of day, do it now if you like, the magic of doing this exercise at night is that it fills you with positive emotions that help you drift off to sleep and wake with a higher level of positive emotions because the last things you thought of before sleep were positive events that you are grateful for.

Say 'YES'

"The oldest, shortest words - 'yes' and 'no' - are those which require the most thought."
Pythagoras, Greek philosopher

The benefit of having a growth mindset is that we are open to learning and growing; to constantly evolving and performing at our best.

One of the greatest ways to have a mindset of growth is to have a *yes* mentality. A *yes* mindset opens us up to creativity, innovation and success. It helps us to listen more as we are saying *yes* to new possibilities and we want and need to hear more about them and this listening and learning allows us to consider more perspectives.

Saying *yes* opens us up to opportunity (maybe even things that we wouldn't have previously considered) and it can even cultivate originality as we say *yes* to doing something before we have considered the logistics of *how* to do it.

Worrying about *how* to do something inevitably holds us back in that place of fear, because the worry of *how* we are going to achieve something outweighs the possibility of *what* we can achieve.

Of course, there is risk with saying *yes*, but is it riskier than saying *no*? Probably not – after all we are not talking about danger here, we are talking about taking risks to push boundaries and empower ourselves and others.

Saying *yes* can give us freedom. It can allow our minds to embrace the possibility that more is available to us; and there is more and we are worthy of receiving it.

What does it take to adopt a *yes* mindset? Being more curious and asking questions rather than objections created by our limits. Ask what the lesson is in something rather than making the decisions about it and most of all, give your self space and time to respond to situations rather than just reacting. With a little time and space we open ourself up to the possibility that *yes* is an option available to us right now.

Let's PERFORM
Exercise #6
"I Can"

Set aside seven minutes. Think of an opportunity or goal ahead of you which you have been hesitant to strive for.

Write down three reasons you are saying *no*. Start the statements with *"I can't because..."*

1.   **I can't because...**
2.   **I can't because...**
3.   **I can't because...**

Now think of the same opportunity but create your *can list.* Start the statements with *"I can because..."*

1.   **I can because...**
2.   **I can because...**
3.   **I can because...**

These are your *YES* statements and they replace the *can't list.*

What can you say *yes* to?

Have Fun

"Fun is only possible if you have a mindset that allows it." Morten Harket, Singer

The best way to not just develop a great and positive mindset but to also be emotionally fitter and protect our mental health is to have fun!

Life can be very serious – becoming and being an adult can be serious - so the more fun we can have the healthier we can be and the more we can achieve.

Of course, some situations demand a sense of seriousness but this doesn't mean we can't play and bring a smile to people's lives through our work and actions. We need a sense of lightness to balance the darkness.

Having fun doesn't mean just messing around though; it means embracing your sense of enjoyment and aligning your strengths with your values and actions.

The more we enjoy something, the more fun we have, the more positive our mindset... and what does a more positive mindset mean? More chance of realizing our intentions, goals and dreams.

There is an upwards cycle that develops from enjoyment and having fun that fuels our mindset to be the most positive it can be. It allows us to see possibilities, allows us to reap rewards, it allows us to connect with others and allows us learn and grow to be the best version of ourselves and PERFORM!

Bringing a sense of fun or play into your life and work may seem at odds with the responsibilities of growing up, but by incorporating that lightness we actually fuel peak performance and enhance our life satisfaction.

What fun and lightness can you choose to bring into your life and work?

Let's PERFORM
Exercise #7
Get Playful!

For seven minutes I want you to get playful and have fun! You can do this any way you choose, but here's some suggestions.

- Watch a comedy sketch or show.
- Learn to juggle.
- Draw a silly picture.
- Dance around your kitchen to music.
- Do some karaoke.
- Pull some funny faces.
- Tell a joke.

How can you factor this sense of fun and play into your everyday life?

"It takes courage to grow up and become who you really are." E. E. Cummings, Poet

My hope for you is that you can now see that what you achieve isn't just about what you do and the actions you take, but it's about how you think about yourself and the possibilities, opportunities and situations that lie ahead of you. Living our best lives and performing at our best is not just about what we do or how we do it; it's more about the way we think about it.

Opting to learn, grow, live abundantly and think positively will help us reach our goals so much quicker than action alone. You have the power and control to choose your mindset to be the best version of yourself. Choose it wisely.

You are enough and you are worthy of the amazing things that lie ahead for you.

Thank you for joining me in this book. Now go and PERFORM and embrace every experience.